FROM HUMDRUM TO HOLY

FROM
HUMDRUM
TO
HOLY

A Step-by-Step Guide to Living Like a Saint

Fr. Ed Broom, O.M.V.

SOPHIA INSTITUTE PRESS
Manchester, New Hampshire

Sophia Institute Press
Box 5284, Manchester, NH 03108
1-800-888-9344

www.SophiaInstitute.com

Sophia Institute Press® is a registered trademark of Sophia Institute.

Library of Congress Cataloging-in-Publication Data

Names: Broom, Ed.
Title: From humdrum to Holy : a step-by-step guide to living like a saint /
    Fr. Ed Broom.
Description: Manchester, New Hampshire : Sophia Institute Press, 2016.
Identifiers: LCCN 2014023546 | ISBN 9781622821983 (pbk. : alk. paper)
Subjects: LCSH: Ignatius, of Loyola, Saint, 1491-1556. Exercitia spiritualia.
    | Spiritual exercises. | Spiritual life—Catholic Church. |
    Holiness—Catholic Church. | Happiness—Religious aspects—Catholic Church.
Classification: LCC BX2179.L8 B768 2016 | DDC 248.3—dc23 LC record available at
http://lccn.loc.gov/2014023546

CONTENTS

Acknowledgments

I would like to thank most especially my mom and dad, Mr. and Mrs. C. E Broom Jr., for their love of God, love of family, love of the priesthood, and love for Jesus and Mary. I would also like to thank Sophia Institute Press for their time, dedication, and zeal in spreading God's word using the most efficacious and modern means of evangelization.

Furthermore, I am greatly indebted to my congregation, the Oblates of the Virgin Mary, and our Founder, Venerable Bruno Lanteri. Thanks to my religious family, I have learned the profound prayer life that comes through the *Spiritual Exercises* of St. Ignatius of Loyola as well as the tender and filial love that Mary has for me and the whole world. My final prayer is that of the psalmist: "Give thanks to the Lord for He is good; His mercy endures forever."

FROM HUMDRUM TO HOLY

1

Building Holiness

Why are we here in this world?

Too many people today are like archers shooting in the dark: bracing their arms, steadying their aim, and letting their arrow sail through the dark with no target in view. Others are like drivers speeding along the freeway, totally oblivious of their destination. It hasn't occurred to them to use a map or a GPS.

If you ask these individuals why we exist and what our purpose on earth is, you'll likely get blank stares and confusion. As spiritual beings, we need to know where we're going and why we're going there. To find these answers, we must begin at the beginning.

Why do we exist? The best answer is found in the famous work *Spiritual Exercises* by St. Ignatius of Loyola, founder of the Jesuits. St. Ignatius offers the clearest and most complete answer: "Man is created to praise, reverence, and serve God our Lord, and by this means to save his soul."[1] St. Ignatius called this definition the "Principle and Foundation" of his *Spiritual Exercises*. In other words, he rightly claims that the entirety of

---

[1] St. Ignatius of Loyola, *Spiritual Exercises*, trans. Louis J. Puhl, S.J. (Chicago: Loyola Press, 1968), no. 23.

our spiritual life is solidly constructed on this short but indispensable statement.

The *Baltimore Catechism* uses similar wording: "God made me to know him, to love him, and to serve him in this life and to be happy with him forever in the next."[2] This was one of the first catechetical truths I learned as a child. It has been seared into my mind, and it has influenced my decisions for more than fifty years. When you, too, meditate on and fully accept the Principle and Foundation, this concept will influence your thought processes and decision-making and will transform your actions into habits that will serve as a motivational force until you take your dying breath. Indeed, every person God has brought into this world as an act of his generous, self-giving love should have this motivational philosophy, which is part of what is known as Ignatian spirituality.

Since understanding this definition is so important to your spiritual journey, let's take some time and examine the details in both formulations.

- *Man is created (God made me).* God does not need us, in the sense that we perform some vital function that he couldn't take care of without us. He is infinitely powerful and totally self-sufficient. He has freely given us life for no other reason than that he simply loves us. What should be our response to this overwhelming and completely selfless love?

- *To know him.* We've all heard the saying "You are what you eat." This is indeed true. Even more importantly,

---

[2] Third Plenary Council of Baltimore, *A Catechism of Christian Doctrine* (1885; Project Gutenberg, 2005) Q. 6, http://www.gutenberg.org/.

however, you are what you *think*. Actions follow a thought process and a decision. Bad actions are preceded by bad thoughts; good actions are preceded by good thoughts. Jesus says that we can know a tree by the fruits it produces (Matt. 12:33). Your thoughts, therefore, ought to be of him.

- *To praise him* in word and deed. St. Augustine reminds us to be sure that our praising the Lord with our lips is not contradicted by the way we live.

- *To reverence him*. Our God is holy, actually *thrice* holy, as portrayed in the vision of the prophet Isaiah in the Temple (Isa. 6:3). Remember that Moses was told to take off his sandals as he stood before the Lord's presence in the burning bush because he was standing on holy ground (Exod. 3:5).

  These are mere symbols of the thrice-holy God we encounter in the Blessed Sacrament, the real presence of Jesus: body, blood, soul, and divinity. Symbol becomes reality in that sublime moment during Mass that we call the Consecration, when man is called to reverence God as did the prophet Isaiah and the humble Moses. Jesus is really and truly present in the holy sacrifice of the Mass and is waiting for us to visit him in his earthly temple, the Blessed Sacrament. Let us reverence and adore him, Emmanuel, "God with us" (Matt. 1:23), in the Eucharist.

- *To serve him*. Our adoration and reverence for Jesus cannot limit itself to our contemplative life but must overflow to our active life. To borrow a phrase from the Ignatian tradition, we should be contemplatives in action. The wisdom of the Thomistic maxim applies here as well: What you have contemplated in the quiet of prayer, share with others. Better to shine on others than to be simply shone upon.

- *And by this means to save our souls and be happy with him forever* — and not just our own souls. One important concept in Ignatian spirituality that helps us build a bridge between contemplation and action is the "Call of the King." The eternal King, our Lord and Savior Jesus Christ, has a very ambitious spiritual enterprise: to conquer and save immortal souls for heaven for all eternity. The essence of true prayer is praising God but also loving what God loves most: the salvation of immortal souls. He calls us to cooperate with Him in this: that is the "Call of the King."

Our praise and reverence for God must bear fruit in a hunger and thirst for the salvation of immortal souls. St. Thomas Aquinas states that one immortal soul has more value than the whole created universe. St. Ignatius's last words as he sent St. Francis Xavier off to India (and eventually to Japan) burned with the same apostolic zeal that had inspired his Principle and Foundation: *Go set the world on fire.*[3] The great St. John Bosco, who manifested his praise and reverence for God by loving and saving youth, summarized his passionate sense of mission with these poignant words: "Give me souls, take away

[3] Raymond A. Schroth, *The American Jesuits* (New York: New York University Press, 2007), 171.

the rest."[4] If we love God, we should love what God loves most: the salvation of the immortal souls that he created to be with him in heaven for all eternity.

So, there is a great deal packed into St. Ignatius's Principle and Foundation. What's more, it is the greatest of challenges to anyone who takes it seriously. Why? It requires the genuine pursuit of the one quality that almost everybody believes is impossible to possess: holiness.

Can you be holy? Yes. That's what this small book is for: to help you become holy, beginning right now, so that you too may go set the world on fire. St. Ignatius of Loyola and his *Spiritual Exercises* will be your guide, and therefore you can be assured that Mary will be too. According to Ignatian tradition, it was the Blessed Virgin Mary who communicated the fundamentals of the *Spiritual Exercises* to St. Ignatius as he prayed in a now-famous cave in Manresa, Spain. Since their completion in 1524, the *Spiritual Exercises* have radically affected thousands of lives and transformed sinners into great saints. Its pages are permeated with the presence of Mary, the Mother of God, the Mother of the Church, and our Mother in the order of grace.

So, as you begin this journey to become holy, let her who is full of grace, the model of contemplation translated into action, the model of a soul absorbed in adoration and reverence for God, lead you to deep sanctity in this life and to the contemplation of the beatific vision of God for all eternity. *Holy Mary, Mother of God, pray for us sinners now and at the hour of our death. Amen.*

---

[4] Ian Mudoch, *Starting Again from Don Bosco* (Bolton, UK: Don Bosco Publications, 2009), 12.

2

God Calls You to Be a Saint

As a young priest starting out my ministry in Buenos Aires, Argentina — the terrain of Pope Francis — I remember once challenging a woman with noble spiritual aspirations with this statement: "You are called to become a saint." She was shocked.

This reaction to the call to sanctity, to become a saint, is not uncommon even among very good Catholics. Why such a startled reaction? Simply put, it would seem that most people have an erroneous concept of sanctity.

In a catechism class, I asked this question: "How many of you want to go to heaven?" All the hands shot up immediately — without a bit of hesitation.

Then I asked the next question: "Now how many of you want to become saints?" Not a single hand rose.

I pointed out the bare truth then, as I do now: all of us are called to become saints because heaven is where God is present, where the angels are present, and where the Blessed Virgin Mary is present. To go to heaven you must become a saint — there is no other way around it.

There are two categories of saints: the canonized, who have been officially proclaimed saints by the Holy Father after approved miracles attributed to them after their death; and the "uncanonized," the huge majority of saints who may not be known to any but God but are still saints.

Becoming a saint requires that we obtain a simple, ardent desire to follow in the footsteps of our Lord and Savior Jesus Christ, the paragon of holiness, and to imitate him. Our holiness flows from union with Christ and the grace that comes from his passion, death, and resurrection. These graces flow most abundantly through his mystical body, the Church, and through the sacraments, especially the most Holy Eucharist, which is truly the body, blood, soul, and divinity of our Lord. When we unite ourselves with Christ, we find that all the virtues that constitute the essence of holiness are truly present in every sacrament because there is Jesus himself.

In the Sermon on the Mount, Jesus challenges us to desire holiness, with these words: "Blessed are those who hunger and thirst for righteousness, for they shall be satisfied" (Matt. 5:6). In the same sermon Jesus launches a command regarding our obligation to become saints: "Be holy as your heavenly Father is holy" (cf. Matt. 5:48). This is not the conditional tense but the *imperative*: Jesus commands us to be holy.

Blessed Teresa of Calcutta reaffirms this commitment in these unequivocal words: "Holiness is not the privilege of the few: it is the simple duty of each of us."[5] The same saint insisted that any young woman who wanted to enter the convent to become a Missionary of Charity had to have an ardent desire to become a saint. Finally, one of the most important documents of Vatican II, the Dogmatic Constitution *Lumen Gentium*, is "the universal call to holiness": all are called to become saints.

---

[5] Kathryn Spink, *The Miracle of Love* (New York: HarperCollins, 1982), 184.

Let us beg our Lady, the Holy Mother of God, that we might have an earnest yearning to become saints and to implement the words of Jesus: "Be holy as your heavenly Father is holy."

3

Ten Ways to Start (or Continue) Becoming a Saint

The call to sainthood isn't really the strange, foreign, and externally imposed standard we may think it is. Remember the words of the psalmist: "As a deer longs for flowing streams, so longs my soul for thee, O God" (cf. Ps. 42:1). The human heart has an insatiable hunger for our Lord. We may try to replace him with food, sex, power, or fame, but these are false gods. They are idols. Deep down, it is really God whom we seek—the one thing necessary.

Don't worry: although Jesus commands us to be holy, that doesn't mean he expects us to grow a halo instantaneously. He knows that holiness has to be learned and lived and practiced. To begin, here are ten simple suggestions (each one starts with the letter M—the first letter in Mary's name):

Morning Prayer
William Shakespeare wrote *All's Well That Ends Well*. Let us give a twist to that famous phrase: "All's well that *begins* well." If you begin your day by offering to Jesus, through Mary, your thoughts,

actions, and prayers, then the rest of your day will go much more smoothly. Here is a traditional Morning Offering:

O Jesus, through the Immaculate Heart of Mary, I offer you my prayers, works, joys, and sufferings of this day for all the intentions of your Sacred Heart, in union with the holy sacrifice of the Mass throughout the world, in reparation for my sins, for the intentions of all my associates, and in particular for the intentions of the Holy Father this month.

That's wind in your sails and a superb start to your day.

Meals

Ask God to bless your meals — and not just dinner, but breakfast and lunch as well. Call to mind how many people in the world do not have enough to eat; how many children this very day will die of hunger; how many, as in the parable of Lazarus and the rich man, long for the scraps that fall from the table (see Luke 16:21). You and I have more than enough, and almost every week we toss excess food into the garbage disposal. Be thankful to your loving and providential Father for the daily bread he gives you.

Meditation on the Bible

Pope Benedict XVI, Pope Francis, and the saints insist that we must immerse ourselves more deeply in the infinite riches of the word of God. God is our heavenly Father, and he wants to feed and nourish us. Therefore, open his Bible every day and read it. Reading it from cover to cover might prove exhausting, so start with the Gospels, or perhaps flip to one of the more famous stories you remember from your childhood: Daniel in the lions' den, Moses leading the people across the Red Sea, Jonah and the whale. Read prayerfully, and you'll see what God is trying to tell you.

Mass and Holy Communion

Even more important than physical bread and even the word of God is the Bread of Life: the body, blood, soul, and divinity of Jesus Christ. While preaching in Capernaum, Jesus proclaimed the necessity of this Bread of Life (see John 6). We might even say it is a matter of life and death — eternal life or eternal death.

Listen to the Master: "I am the Bread of Life.... [H]e who eats my flesh and drinks my blood has eternal life, and I will raise him up at the last day" (John 6:48, 54). In other words, if we want to live eternally, we must nourish our souls frequently with the body and blood of our Lord. Holy Communion in the context of Holy Mass is our key to sharing life with our Lord for eternity.

Mercy toward Others

Another condition for entering the Kingdom of God is mercy. If we want to receive the Lord's mercy, we must be merciful to others. The Our Father could not be clearer: "Forgive us our trespasses *as we forgive those who trespass against us.*"

Jesus, of course, is our model. Even from the Cross he offers us two lessons in mercy. In the first case, he says: "*Father, forgive* them, for they know not what they do" (Luke 23:34, emphasis added). Then, to the repentant thief, he says, "Truly, I say to you, today you will be with me *in Paradise*" (Luke 23:43, emphasis added). Here we see the triumph of God's mercy in the last moment.

The *Diary* of St. Faustina tells us that Jesus exhorts all to perform at least one act of mercy every day. It can be done in one of three ways: prayer for someone, kind words, or some kind deed. Let us take seriously Jesus' words: "Be merciful even as your Father is merciful" (Luke 6:36).

Manners in Church

Pope Benedict sadly reminded the modern world that we have lost the sense of the sacred and the sense of mystery, especially in church. Moses took off his sandals before the burning bush; he understood that divine holiness requires certain proper behavior. We must rediscover the holiness of our thrice-holy God, especially in church, where Jesus is truly present in the Blessed Sacrament. Let these beautiful words help you keep in mind the reason for good manners in church: "O Sacrament most holy, O Sacrament divine, all praise and all thanksgiving be every moment thine."

Meekness and Gentleness of Heart

An authentic manifestation of holiness is reflected by meekness. Meekness is not weakness but rather a powerful virtue. It brings under control "anger and its disorderly effects" and "every inordinate movement of resentment at another person's character or behavior."[6] We have no better model of this virtue than Jesus himself, who stated, "Come to me, all you that labor, and are burdened, and I will refresh you. Take up my yoke upon you, and learn of me, because I am meek, and humble of heart: and you shall find rest to your souls. For my yoke is sweet and my burden light" (Matt. 11:28–30, Douay-Rheims).

Jesus, meek and humble of heart, make my heart like unto thine.

---

[6] John A. Hardon, S.J, *Pocket Catholic Dictionary* (New York: Image, 1985), s.v. "meekness."

Master Jesus, Our Heavenly Model

We all need models on which to pattern our lives, so let Jesus be your model. "I am the way, and the truth, and the life," he said (John 14:6). By reading and meditating on the Gospels, you will discover in Jesus' words and example the way to lead a holy life.

Mission

An authentic follower of Christ is a prophet and an evangelizer. Both Pope Benedict XVI and Pope Francis have insistently reminded us that we must experience a personal and deep relationship with Jesus as our true friend. But this treasure must be shared with others, just as Andrew ran to tell Peter about Jesus (John 1:41) and the Samaritan woman at the well ran to tell her compatriots that she had found the Messiah (John 4:28–29). Like our Lady, who hastened to share Jesus with her cousin Elizabeth (Luke 1:39ff.), we must joyfully bring the gospel to the whole world. Our Lord's last words in the Gospel of St. Matthew are: "Go therefore and make disciples of all nations, baptizing them in the name of the Father and of the Son and of the Holy Spirit, teaching them to observe all that I have commanded you; and lo, I am with you always, to the close of the age" (Matt. 28:19–20).

Mary Most Holy and the Rosary

St. Louis de Montfort's many great teachings can be summed up: whenever we find our spiritual progression to be lacking, we will also find that we are also lacking in bringing Mary into our spiritual lives.[7] Mary is, indeed, the quickest, easiest, most efficacious path to Jesus.

---

[7] Cf. St. Louis de Montfort, *True Devotion to Mary*, trans. F. W. Faber (Charlotte, NC: TAN Books, 2010).

When our Lady appeared at Fátima six times in 1917, she said each time: Pray the rosary. When a mother repeats herself, it is because her message is important. If our heavenly Mother Mary has exhorted us repeatedly to pray the rosary, it must be of prime importance for the salvation of our souls and the salvation of the world.

Pope St. John Paul II encouraged Catholics to pray the rosary, especially in the family, and for two reasons: for world peace and for the safeguarding of the family.[8] This echoes the immortal words of the Rosary Priest, Fr. Patrick Peyton: "The family that prays together stays together. A world at prayer is a world at peace."[9]

Let us all accept the challenge to strive for holiness. If we make a firm decision to become a saint, we can help to change the world for the better.

Holy Mary, Mother of God, pray for us always.

---

[8] John Paul II, apostolic letter *Rosarius Virginis Mariae* ("The Rosary of the Virgin Mary"), October 16, 2002, no. 39.
[9] Patrick Peyton, *Father Peyton's Rosary Prayer Book* (San Francisco: Ignatius Press, 2003), 21.

4

Self-Knowledge

We all know Clark Kent and his double life — as mild-mannered reporter and Superman. As Superman he is invincible, Samson-like, and superior to any first-class athlete. However, exposure to one element — kryptonite — would cause his downfall.

Spiritual writers insist on the necessity of self-knowledge. A famous aphorism of the desert Fathers was just two short words: *know thyself.* Even the classical Greek philosopher Socrates asserted: "The life that is not examined is a life not worth living."[10] Fortunately, St. Ignatius of Loyola has bequeathed to the Church and to the world at large the classical Rules for Discernment, "for perceiving and knowing in some manner the different movements in the soul — the good, to receive them, and the bad to reject them."[11] These Rules for Discernment — as well as the *Spiritual Exercises'* Two Standards and Daily Examen — insist on self-knowledge as an indispensable tool for growth in holiness.

This chapter will focus on the fourteenth rule for discernment, which I call the kryptonite rule. First, I will present some simple

[10] Plato, *Apology,* ed. John M. Cooper (Indianapolis: Hackett, 1997), 37e–38a.
[11] See St. Ignatius of Loyola, *Spiritual Exercises*, no. 313.

analogies and will then explain how to discover weaknesses and to act valiantly so as not to collapse in the spiritual contest.

Baseball Analogy

In sports, team members study their opponents in various ways. One way is to detect the weak point of a player or of the whole team and to take advantage of this weakness. At times the knowledge of one weak point of a team or an opponent can make the difference between victory and defeat.

In baseball, the primary goal of the pitcher is to eliminate the batter. In what ways? The pitcher will use all his ingenuity and skill to get the batter to pop out, ground out, fly out, and—best yet—strike out. Today professional pitchers and teams have videos of the opposing players that they study before the game. From these videos they can detect where the batter's weak points are.

Maybe the batter can pound a fastball into the seats. If that is the case, a good pitcher will throw an off-speed pitch—a curve-ball, a slider, a sinker, or a changeup. If the batter can hit a ball on the inside corner, the pitcher will try to pinpoint the ball out and away, almost nicking the outside corner.

The strategy of baseball is unique and intricate and demands time, reflection, observation, and determination. Excellent pitchers have the ability to throw the ball well, but also to outthink the batter.

Military Analogy

In rule fourteen of the *Spiritual Exercises*, St. Ignatius offers us another analogy by way of military expertise and strategy. The Spanish saint and expert in spiritual discernment catapults us back to the Middle Ages, when feudal forts and castles abounded. These castles and forts had to be constructed in such a way that enemies could not enter, penetrate, and plunder the building. An enemy would study the fortress diligently. Having detected an opening, a crack, a leak, a hole in the wall, an open door or gate, or an exposed lattice, he would mercilessly force himself upon the structure so as to capture it.

St. Teresa of Ávila, in her classic, *Interior Castle*, presents the interior life of prayer in terms of a castle with various levels or stories. Surrounding the castle is a moat in which there are ugly reptiles, turtles, snakes, and alligators to intimidate any person who might seek entrance.

All these images — of sports, military fortresses and castles, and kryptonite — are meant to illustrate how a weakness in our soul can subject us to harm. So let us identify our weaknesses, which expose us to the vicious attack of Satan. St. Ignatius calls Satan *the enemy of our human nature*.

Desolation

When you find yourself in a state of desolation, meaning sadness, depression, lack of faith, hope, and charity, you might simply feel that life has no real meaning and nobody seems to care about you. What is the purpose of this dreary and bleak existence? We all go through this state of soul — at times anyway — and it is a prime opportunity for the devil to see our weaknesses exposed and launch his deadly weapons. Be prepared for his attack in the state of desolation.

Laziness in Prayer

Another weakness that gives the devil opportunity is when our prayer life declines. For example, the apostles in the Garden of Olives abandoned Jesus when he most needed their presence and friendship. Instead of accompanying him in prayer, they fell asleep. The devil took advantage of this, and they fell when Jesus was arrested. Peter denied him three times and the others fled. Lack of prayer exposes all of us to temptation.

Sickness

The devil takes advantage of all occasions and circumstances. He does not respect our state of health. On the contrary, seeing our bodies weak and depleted by physical maladies, he can become more aggressive in aiming and launching his spiritual bombs, hoping for our moral collapse. Even when our body is sick, our soul must make a concerted effort not to give up on prayer. What air is to our lungs, prayer is to our soul and to our salvation.

Failures

Failures of any size or form can cast us into a state of desolation. Economic setbacks, relational tensions, family altercations and fights, academic failures— these can all cause extreme turmoil in our souls and result in desolation and thus give the devil a chance to shoot for the kill.

Secrecy of Soul

When the individual is being tested by a state of desolation, the devil has another trick. This time it is *secrecy*. While the person's inner turmoil rises to a boiling point, the devil, never one to rest when he sees an opportunity to attack, convinces the person in this dark state to clam up and not reveal to anybody his state of soul. Then the devil enters and blows everything out of proportion. St. Ignatius, in the thirteenth rule for discernment insists that this tormented soul battered right and left by interior turmoil should seek out a confessor or spiritual director and lay bare his soul. This will frustrate the devil and his plans. Secrecy of soul — that is, not opening up to the confessor — is a weakness that the devil utilizes with consummate perfection in many souls.

To advance on the highway of holiness, to ascend the mountain of heroic virtue, to triumph in spiritual warfare, to fight the good fight and run the good race and receive the crown of victory, it is of paramount importance that we strive to know ourselves better. Get to know what your own kryptonite is. Get to know where it is, when it draws close to you and how to flee from it. If you do this, the victory will be yours in time and for all eternity.

5

Make a Plan of Life

One of the concrete manifestations of goodwill toward God and of a desire to grow in holiness through prayer and through living with what St. Ignatius called "a magnanimous spirit"[12] is to formulate and write out a plan of life in a clear, methodical, and practical way.

We belong to a God of order, so a successful plan of life will bring order to whatever is disordered in our lives. That is no small project. Both original sin and actual sin have left our lives marked by upheaval, confusion, and disorder. It is time to let God arrange our lives, just as Our Lady of Guadalupe gently arranged all of those beautiful roses in the tilma of St. Juan Diego.

First, I recommend that you choose a specific yearlong theme for your plan of life. Here are a few suggestions:

- Choose a corporal or spiritual work of mercy that you feel God is challenging you to embrace and live out this year.[13]

---

[12] *Spiritual Exercises*, no. 5.

[13] The Corporal Works of Mercy are these: to feed the hungry, to give drink to the thirsty, to clothe the naked, to shelter the homeless, to visit the sick, to visit the imprisoned, and to bury

* Focus on *one* of the fourteen Stations of the Cross.

* Choose one of the eight Beatitudes found in Matthew 5:1–12, and strive to live it.

* Adopt a Marian theme, such as one of the Mysteries of the Rosary.

* Select a biblical verse or scene that captivates your attention, such as Jesus walking on the water or one of his seven last words from the Cross.[14]

* Take as your theme the simple words of the Divine Mercy image: "Jesus, I trust in You."

Once you have established a theme for your plan of life, honestly examine certain areas of your life that need improvement, and come up with a short, practical proposal for improving them. The key words here are *short* and *practical*. Too many people (with good intentions) create overly ambitious programs for themselves that they abandon within the first week.

Remember the words of Jesus: "He who is faithful in a very little is faithful also in much" (Luke 16:10). The essence of the

---

the dead. The Spiritual Works of Mercy are these: to admonish the sinner, to instruct the ignorant, to counsel the doubtful, to comfort the sorrowful, to bear wrongs patiently, to forgive all injuries, and to pray for the living and the dead.

[14] The seven last words of Jesus are these: "Father, forgive them; for they know not what they do" (Luke 23:34); "Truly, I say to you, today you will be with me in Paradise" (Luke 23:43); "Woman, behold, your son!... Behold, your mother!" (John 19:26, 27); "My God, my God, why hast thou forsaken me?" (Matt. 27:46); "I thirst" (John 19:28); "It is finished" (John 19:30); "Father, into thy hands I commit my spirit!" (Luke 23:46).

spirituality of St. Thérèse is to do these small, ordinary things in one's daily life with extraordinary love, which is the secret and key to holiness.

Here are some areas for you to consider in making your plan of life:

Prayer

Examine seriously your prayer life and pray about how you can improve it. Do you often rush through prayers without thinking about the God to whom you are praying? Do you forget that you are not merely reciting old formulas but are actually addressing a Person — three Persons, in fact? Part of the problem might be that you are not making enough time to pray so that when you do find the time, you are out of practice and rush through it. Would you rush through a conversation with an old friend or skip over details? Of course not.

> *Action*: Decide to give God just five extra minutes of prayer every day. Find a quiet place to pray, and slow down; take a breath between each sentence or even sit in silence for a few minutes. Make a list of your intentions and don't forget to express gratitude and thanksgiving.

Confession

We are all sinners. Sin is mortal enemy number one, and until our dying day we must fight fiercely against it. One of the most efficacious ways to conquer sin is through the sacrament of confession, in which we receive God's healing touch and grace.

> *Action*: Go to confession *more frequently* (you can decide how often). Prepare for confession the night before, and trust more in God's mercy.

Mass and Holy Communion

Our eternal salvation depends on our allowing Jesus to save us. Read and meditate on Jesus' "bread of life" discourse (John 6:22–71), in which he outlines clearly what we must do to be saved. Adam and Eve brought death to the world through an act of eating. Jesus promises us eternal life through eating and drinking his body and blood in Holy Communion. He states clearly: "I am the bread of life.... [H]e who eats my flesh and drinks my blood has eternal life, and I will raise him up at the last day" (John 6:48, 54).

> *Action*: Aim to attend Mass and receive Holy Communion daily. If this is already your practice, come ten minutes before Mass and offer your intentions, depositing them on the altar. The graces that flow from the Eucharist into your heart are in direct proportion to your preparation and disposition. One Holy Communion could transform you into a saint.

Apostolic Life

To be a follower of Christ is to evangelize. In the last verses of the Gospel of Matthew, Jesus commands, "Go therefore and make disciples of all nations ... teaching them to observe all that I have commanded you; and lo, I am with you always, to the close of the age" (Matt. 28:19–20). So while we are indeed challenged every day to grow in faith, we are also expected to share that faith with others. In fact, sharing your faith is one of the best ways to fortify it.

> *Action*: Pray the rosary with your family every day. Also, invite a fallen-away Catholic back home to the Catholic Church. If we love God, we should love what God loves — the salvation of souls.

Permanent Formation

Our Catholic Faith is a fathomless ocean, and Catholics must make a concerted effort to learn that Faith more deeply. For this reason, Pope Benedict XVI dedicated October 2012 to November 2013 as a Year of Faith and exhorted Catholics to read the documents of Vatican II, especially the four Dogmatic Constitutions: *Dei Verbum* (on the Word of God), *Sacrosanctum Concilium* (on the Liturgy), *Gaudium et Spes* and *Lumen Gentium* (documents on the Church in the modern world). Studying the *Catechism of the Catholic Church* is another great way to understand the Faith better. These sources teach us not only the truths of the Faith but how to live them out.

> *Action*: Set aside at least fifteen minutes every day to study your Catholic Faith.

Penance

A bird needs two wings to fly. Likewise, to soar high in the spiritual atmosphere, we need the two "wings" of prayer and penance. Our Lady of Fátima, who appeared to three shepherd children, insisted that they pray — especially the most holy rosary — and offer up sacrifices for the conversion of sinners. We should all make acts of penance for our own sins and those of others.

> *Action*: The Church calls us to do some form of penance on Fridays. Choose one of the following penances to practice on Fridays: abstain from eating meat or sweets for the day; eat less on that day; fast from watching television; make the Stations of the Cross; do not complain the whole day.

Work

All of us are called to work. God told Adam that he would earn his bread by the sweat of his face (cf. Gen. 3:19). We all know (probably from personal experience) that idleness can lead to sin. Examine carefully your daily work and look for areas for improvement.

> *Action*: Be punctual in starting, hard in working, and honest about the time you put in. Remember that you are working for our Lord. As St. Paul reminds us, "So, whether you eat or drink, or whatever you do, do all to the glory of God" (1 Cor. 10:31).

Vocational Call

It is an unfortunate fact today that while the training and preparation given to aspiring priests and religious is ample, it is lacking for those called to the married life. If you are in the latter group, consider how you can be a better wife or husband and a better parent. Do you put Christ first in your marriage and family? If not, what can you do to correct that today? Pray over this, and the Holy Spirit will inspire you with a concrete proposal.

> *Action*: Pray as a family. Say a prayer with your spouse before you start your day, asking God to guide you both. You can also involve your children in prayer by praying a decade of the rosary as a family after dinner or while driving to Mass.

Spiritual Direction

In addition to frequent confession, spiritual reading, and serious theological studies, those who are pursuing the path of perfection should have some form of periodic spiritual direction. St. John of the Cross put it bluntly: "He who has himself as spiritual director has an idiot for a disciple." In other words we all have blind spots and need someone other than ourselves to help us on the demanding and rigorous path to becoming a saint.

Action: Pray that God will help you to find this guide. If you have already discovered one, be thankful, humble, docile, and obedient.

Mary: Our Life, Our Sweetness, and Our Hope

A plan of life would be incomplete if Mary were left out of it. The quickest, easiest, and most efficacious path to holiness is through true devotion to Mary. She is the shortcut to God.

Action: Choose a way to make Mary part of your daily life: pray the rosary daily; make St. Louis de Montfort's consecration to Mary; read about Mary; live in the presence of Mary and in imitation of her virtue; identify your weakest virtue, and ask Mary to help you grow stronger in it.

Let us conclude with words of wisdom taken from Adolphe Tanquerey's classic, *The Spiritual Life*:

The man who holds to a well-defined rule of life saves considerable time: (1) He wastes no time in hesitation. He knows exactly what he is to do and when he is to do it. Even if his schedule is not mathematically detailed, at least it sets off time-periods and lays down principles with regard to religious exercises, recreation, work, etc.... (2) There is little or nothing unforeseen, for even should the unusual occur, he has already provided for it by determining beforehand exercises that may be shortened and the manner of making up for them. At all events, as soon as these exceptional circumstances cease to exist, he immediately comes back to his rule. (3) Inconstancy likewise vanishes. The rule urges him to do always what is prescribed, and that every day and at every hour of the day. Thus the habits are formed that give continuity to his life and assure perseverance; his days are full days, teeming with good works and merits.[15]

[15] Adolphe Tanquerey, *The Spiritual Life: A Treatise on Ascetical and Mystical Theology* (Charlotte, NC: TAN Books, 2001), nos. 560, 205.

6

What Is Your Soul Worth?

"For what shall it profit a man, if he shall gain the whole world, and lose his own soul? Or what shall a man give in exchange for his soul?" (Mark 8:36–37, KJV). Consider your soul for a moment: what, according to Jesus, is it worth?

It's simple: all the money, possessions, houses, mountains, oceans, animals — indeed, *all of creation itself* is not worth as much as *your* immortal soul. Your immortal soul has infinite value. Everything in the created world is not equal to just one immortal soul.

Take a moment to contemplate the beauty of nature. The beautiful blue skies, the pure white clouds, the multicolored leaves in autumn, the snowcapped mountains, the brilliant and bright rainbow crossing the horizon in a lovely arc, the powerful waves crashing endlessly on the shore, the majestic eagle soaring in the heights, and the sky painted with a multitude of lights — all of these natural phenomena are a mere glimmer of the majestic beauty and greatness of one immortal soul. In fact, St. Catherine of Siena was once granted a vision of one soul in the state of grace, and she fell to her knees in ecstasy, stunned by its glaring beauty.

A powerful proof of the infinite value of one immortal soul is the apostolic zeal that motivated the saints in their heroic efforts to save souls. For instance, the Curé of Ars, St. John Vianney (1786–1859), spent between thirteen and eighteen hours in the confessional day and night, in the cold of winter and the blistering heat and humidity of the summer, hearing the confessions of sinners. Why? For one simple reason: love for God and love for what God loves most—the salvation of immortal souls. The Curé ate only two or three potatoes a day, slept only three hours a night, battled constantly with the devil, and scourged himself to the point of bloodshed and weeping, all for the love of God and love for immortal souls. The patron of parish priests knew keenly the value of a soul reconciled to God through the blood of Christ.

It was for the salvation of immortal souls that St. Padre Pio of Pietrelcina (1887–1968) willingly accepted the stigmata. In 1918, while he was absorbed in prayer, his hands, feet, and side were pierced with the wounds of the crucified Lord. Jesus promised this modern saint that he would bear this stigmata and the excruciating pain that went with it for fifty long years and then at the end of his life it would disappear. We can be sure that many souls have benefited from this heroic sacrifice.

Why did the three little shepherds of Fátima—Lucia, Francisco, and Jacinta—willingly accept difficulties and make constant sacrifices that entailed great suffering, even though they were mere children? It was because of their love for Jesus and for Mary and for the salvation of immortal souls. The sacrifices that these children underwent at such a tender age shows the power of the Holy Spirit in the lives of generous souls. After seeing a graphic vision of hell, Jacinta Marto, the youngest of the three seers at Fátima, sacrificed dancing, which she had always loved, in order to help save souls from such a fate. She gave up her favorite food, the sweet grapes of the Portuguese hillsides. Along with her two cousins, she wore around her waist a rough rope that caused her discomfort during the day. She prayed with her forehead to the ground, a penitential posture. All three children, but especially Jacinta, prayed the rosary fervently many times, without wearying of it. Why? They did all this to help save souls from going to hell and to bring them safely home to heaven.

Among the holy men and women who knew the value of souls and strove to bring them salvation is St. Maria Faustina Kowalska. Her magnificent *Diary* tells how Jesus revealed to her his love for souls. However, Jesus pointed out that love for the salvation of souls is measured by the willingness to suffer for these souls.

The source from which the saints' love flows is the blood of Jesus. The word of God reveals most poignantly the value of souls in that, on Calvary, Jesus shed his precious blood for every soul: "And if you invoke as Father him who judges each one impartially according to his deeds, conduct yourselves with fear throughout the time of your exile. You know that you were ransomed from the futile ways inherited from your fathers, not with perishable things such as silver or gold, but *with the precious blood of Christ*, like that of a lamb without blemish or spot" (1 Pet. 1:17–19, emphasis added).

It can't be overstated: if you were the only person created in the whole universe, Jesus would have shed every drop of his most precious blood for your immortal soul. How valuable indeed your soul is in the eyes of Almighty God.

7

Improve Your Prayer Life

How much time and energy is exerted in obtaining a degree from a prestigious university? How much blood, sweat, and tears are expended to win a trophy in some sporting event or to organize a surprise birthday party? If we can invest so much time, money, and emotional and physical energy in such natural pursuits, should we not at least consider doing more for what has been called "the art of all arts": the practice of prayer?

Prayer has traditionally been defined as "the lifting of the mind and heart to God," and learning to lift ourselves up to God is the key to salvation.[16] Following are five steps you can undertake to improve your prayer life, grow in holiness, be a source of holiness to others, and experience greater peace and joy.

Conviction

First, we must be convinced of the importance of prayer in our lives and for our eternal salvation. St. Alphonsus expresses it starkly: "He who prays will be saved; he who does not pray will

---

[16] John F. O'Grady, *The Roman Catholic Church: Its Origin and Nature* (New York: Paulist Press, 1997), 97.

be damned."[17] St. Robert Bellarmine has a catchy way of expressing the indispensable character of prayer: "Let us then explain the conditions of praying well so that we may learn to pray well, live well, and die well."[18]

A final, easy analogy: as air is to the lungs, so must prayer be to our soul. When there is no air for the lungs, death arrives quickly. Likewise, a person who does not pray can easily fall prey to temptation, fall into mortal sin, and lose out on God's friendship.

Confession

If we are not at peace with God, if our conscience is reproaching us over unconfessed and unforgiven sins, prayer will be difficult. God is our friend, and if we hurt him, we ought to apologize, seek forgiveness, and return to amicable relations.

Set Times to Pray

You can pray at any time and in any place or circumstance. However, there are prime times for praying. Morning prayer upon arising from sleep, grace before meals, prayer before going on a trip, the family rosary in the evening, and night prayers — these are traditional times for prayer.

Mass and Holy Communion

By far, the greatest prayer in the world is the holy sacrifice of the Mass. Sunday Mass is obligatory, under pain of mortal sin. If we

---

[17] Cf. Alphonsus Liguori, *Prayer: The Great Means of Salvation and of Perfection*, ed. Paul A. Boer (Seattle: CreateSpace, 2012), 26.

[18] St. Robert Bellarmine, *Robert Bellarmine, Spiritual Writing*, trans. Roland J. Teske (Mahwah, NJ: Paulist Press, 1988), 264.

truly love God, however, we should aim not for the minimum but for the maximum. The greatest action and gesture under the heavens is to assist at Holy Mass and receive Holy Communion fervently, humbly, and with great confidence. The angels in heaven experience a holy envy toward us because even the greatest of angels cannot receive Jesus in Holy Communion. How privileged we are.

Seek Our Lady of the Rosary

The rosary is our means of offering flowers to Mary, the Mother of God. The family should find a time and place and pray the rosary every day. May the father, who is the spiritual head of the family, initiate this practice, bring the family together, and persevere in this prayer for the salvation of his entire family.

If we implement these five practices into our personal prayer lives, we will bring forth fruit in abundance. May Our Lady of Grace inspire us to strive for daily growth in our prayer lives.

8

The Hour of Power

The effects of a daily Holy Hour are countless.

The person who seriously makes the decision to make a daily Holy Hour—that is, to spend an hour in prayer in front of the Blessed Sacrament, in a church or in an adoration chapel—to be faithful to it with a mighty determination, to struggle through it on tough days, and to persevere until the end will have a crown of glory in heaven after having done enormous good on earth. Many people are often very busy and are not sure how they can find a whole hour to pray and meditate. By slowly adopting this habit, however, adding a few minutes of prayer each day, even the busiest people eventually find that they just can't go a single day without their Holy Hour and the many joys it brings them.

One notable and highly compelling proponent of the daily Holy Hour was the Venerable Archbishop Fulton J. Sheen. Although Archbishop Sheen was a preacher, a writer, and a famous television and radio host, he was also a man of God who refused to attribute his successes to himself. Rather, he attributed his success to Jesus, whom he met each day in the Blessed Sacrament during his Holy Hour. Sheen called it "the Hour of Power." He once stated that in his fifty years as a priest (and many years as a bishop), he never missed making even *one* Holy Hour.

Consider some of the many fruits of faithfulness to the daily Holy Hour:

Friendship with Christ

Pope Benedict XVI constantly challenged us to strive to cultivate an ever-deepening friendship with Jesus. At the Last Supper, Jesus called his apostles "friends" (John 15:15), but he also calls *you* to a deep friendship with him. We all seek friendship and union with others. Obviously, Jesus is the best of friends; he is the faithful friend who will never fail us.

True friendship, however, must be cultivated by spending time with a friend, visiting him, getting to know him, sharing your joys and sorrows, failures and successes. We can always express our inmost thoughts to Jesus, no matter how anguished we are, and he will understand us down to the minutest detail.

The Depths of the Word of God

While in the presence of Christ in the Eucharist during your Holy Hour, why not read the word of God? "Man shall not live by *bread alone*, but by every word that proceeds from the mouth of God" (Matt. 4:4, emphasis added). The Holy Hour is the perfect time to open your Bible and read, meditate, listen, and let your heart be moved by the Lord. The quiet time and the presence of the Eucharist will enlighten you to the power of scripture.

Discipline

Notice the change in your life. The discipline of being faithful to your Holy Hour leads to greater discipline in the other activities in the course of the day. It will help you live a well-ordered and disciplined life in general.

Peace and Harmony

With discipline comes peace. What is peace? St. Augustine defines peace as "the tranquillity of order."[19] Ordering the disordered is the very purpose of St. Ignatius's *Spiritual Exercises*. If you *want* Jesus to calm the storms in your life, come to Him in a Holy Hour.

Work: More Done and Better Done

Many of us complain about lack of time to carry out our various duties in life. Often it is because of the lack of order previously mentioned. The Holy Hour helps us to carry out our daily obligations with more willpower and with greater peace and joy. Jesus himself becomes the secret companion walking with us along the highway of life to eternity — as he walked with the disciples on the road to Emmaus (Luke 24:13–35). He does most of the work, just as he promised: "Come to me, all who labor and are heavy laden, and I will give you rest. Take my yoke upon you, and learn from me, for I am gentle and lowly in heart, and you will find rest for your souls. For my yoke is easy, and my burden is light" (Matt. 11:28–30). It is best to do your daily Holy Hour as early as possible so that Jesus may give you rest before you begin your day and may lighten all your burdens.

Family Conversion and Sanctification

Many of us have family members who have abandoned the Faith, have walked away, and are angry, bitter, and even antagonistic toward all that is related to God. Maybe we have talked to them

---

[19] St Augustine, *Politicial Writings*, trans. Michael W. Tkacz and Douglas Kries, ed. Ernest L. Fortin and Douglas Kries (Indianapolis: Hackett 2004), 154.

and tried to convince them by the best of arguments but have gotten nowhere with them. Often what is lacking is prayer. Jesus said that some devils can be expelled only through prayer and fasting. Offering your daily Holy Hour for the conversion and salvation of your loved ones can prove exceedingly fruitful. Remember St. Monica's many tears and hours of prayer for the conversion of her son St. Augustine.

Fervent Communions

Not only does the daily Holy Hour serve to motivate lost sheep to return to the Good Shepherd, but this personal encounter with the Lord also improves and enhances our reception of Jesus in Holy Communion.

The greatest act we can perform on earth is to receive Jesus in Holy Communion. The better our preparation, the more efficacious will the effects of Holy Communion be in our soul. May our daily Holy Hours transform us into the one we receive in Holy Communion. We remember the words of St. Paul: "It is no longer I who live, but Christ who lives in me" (Gal. 2:20).

Consolation

In the midst of the storms of life, we can always find refuge in our daily Holy Hour. There are days when the battle is fierce, the tug of the passions remains insistent, the devil's attacks are relentless, and the seduction of the world and its values are alluring. How consoling it is to know that Jesus is always waiting for us to come and seek true refuge in his Sacred Heart and in the Immaculate Heart of Mary.

Sacred Heart of Jesus, I trust in you. Sweet heart of Mary, be my salvation.

Good Example

Before He ascended into heaven, Jesus commissioned His disciples, and us, to go out to the whole world and proclaim the good news (Matt. 28:19–20), but the word that we preach must be supported by the example of our lives. The person who makes the daily Holy Hour radiates goodness and inspires others to follow the same path. At the end of his life, Venerable Fulton Sheen decided to preach retreats to priests and bishops with one goal in mind: to convince them to make the firm commitment to make a daily Holy Hour. He knew better than anyone that if they made this with determination, they would become living examples of Christ, who would transform lives, parishes, dioceses, and the world.

Heaven

Union with the Father, the Son, and the Holy Spirit and with Mary and the angels and saints for all eternity in heaven is the goal and the most sublime fruit of the daily Holy Hour. Recall those words: "Let us then explain the conditions of praying well so that we may learn to pray well, live well, and die well."[20] Our Holy Hour is but a glimpse of the eternity we will share with Jesus if we cling to him as we learn to do in our short Hour of Power.

In sum, right now let us make the firm commitment to the daily Holy Hour. If you are faithful to a daily Holy Hour, you will grow in friendship with Jesus, grow in holiness and peace

---

[20] *Robert Bellarmine, Spiritual Writing,* trans. Roland J. Teske (Mahwah, NJ: Paulist Press, 1988), 264.

of soul, work well and with order and discipline, be a source of sanctification and conversion, receive Jesus with greater purity of heart in Holy Communion, and, most importantly, contemplate the beauty of the unveiled face of Jesus for all eternity.

9

Four Ways to Increase Patience

Patience is so important that Jesus Christ, our model in all virtues, said: "In your patience you shall possess your souls" (Luke 21:19, Douay-Rheims). One pious soul prayed in desperation: "Lord, give me patience right now!" Maybe this has been your prayer for the last few years.

Our patience can be tested by various circumstances: the failure of health, economic setbacks, family members who could put the holy Job to the test, weather extremes, failed and broken relationships, and *even God*—when it seems as if he is distant, that he does not hear our prayers or at least seems indifferent to our pleadings.

How, then, can we acquire the all-important virtue of patience that, as Jesus reminds us, is necessary for the salvation of our immortal souls? Here are four ways to do so.

Persevere in Begging for Help.

St. Ignatius of Loyola insists that we must beg for grace, and St. Augustine humbly reminds us that we are all beggars before God. God is willing to give if we simply persevere in asking him. Remember the persistent widow who gained the favor of the callous and cold-hearted judge for the simple reason that she kept begging for his help (see Luke 18:1–8)? "Ask, and it will be given you; seek, and you will find; knock, and it will be opened to you" (Matt. 7:7).

Follow Jesus' Example.

There is a saying: "Tell me with whom you associate, and I will tell you who you are." Reading the Gospels and meditating on the words, gestures, and actions of Jesus can help us to become like him. Spend time with Jesus in the Gospels and associate with him more and more. You will start to imitate Jesus, especially in the virtue of patience.

Meditate on the Passion of Christ.

When trials descend on you, call to mind some element of the passion of Christ, either from the Gospels or from the works of writers such as Anne Catherine Emmerich. This will put your trials into a broader and supernatural perspective: the trials you suffer might indeed be very painful, but compared with what our Lord has gone through, they are a mere trifle. Also, we suffer trials partially as a result of our own sinfulness, but Jesus suffered the most excruciating pains even as the epitome of innocence. Choose one element or detail of the passion that strikes you most, and recall this scene when your patience is put to the bitter test. The love of Jesus can move you to carry patiently the most burdensome crosses. As St. Paul states: "The love of Christ urges us on" (cf. 2 Cor. 5:14).

Pray to Mary, Our Lady of Sorrows.

One essential element in Mel Gibson's *The Passion of the Christ* was the presence of the Blessed Virgin Mary throughout the film. The intensity of Mary's suffering was second only to Jesus'.

The film portrays Our Lady of Sorrows along the way of Calvary accompanying Jesus in his most bitter trial. Mary stood at the foot of the Cross, patient to a heroic degree. She practiced patience her whole life: traveling to Bethlehem, fleeing to Egypt, seeking out her lost son for three long days, losing her beloved husband, St. Joseph, to death, and accompanying Jesus, seeing him crucified, and staying with him until he drew his last breath. When our patience is put to the test, then, we should lift our minds, hearts, and souls to our Lady, and she will acquire for us heroic patience.

We all struggle to be patient with others, with ourselves, with circumstances, and at times even with God. Let us use the weapons we have in our arsenal to attain the all-important virtue of patience. Let us pray as beggars to the most generous giver, God. Let us follow the example of Jesus. Let us meditate on his passion and, when opportunities to practice patience surface, call to mind all that Jesus suffered for us. Finally, let us ask Our Lady of Sorrows to obtain for us meek, humble, and patient hearts.

10

Be Pure

The sixth beatitude is "Blessed are the pure in heart, for they shall see God" (Matt. 5:8).

If we wish to be holy, our goal must be to see God and to perceive his will clearly. For that, we need our physical eyes and the eyes of our soul to be sanctified. The proverb "The eyes are the mirror of the soul" expresses this truth.

So, for instance, Jesus tells us: "You have heard that it was said, 'You shall not commit adultery.' But I say to you that every one who looks at a woman lustfully has already committed adultery with her in his heart" (Matt. 5:27–28).

Job, the holy and afflicted man of the Old Testament, asserted with conviction: "I have made a covenant with my eyes; how then could I look upon a virgin?" (Job 31:1).

The great King David, after spying on Bathsheba, committed adultery with her, which led to murder and denial. In the book of Daniel, the lecherous elders tried to calumniate Susanna, an innocent and chaste married woman. Both King David and the elders fell headlong into these mires of immorality for one specific reason: they failed to keep custody of their eyes.

What we see becomes engraved in our mind; from the mind it descends to our emotions and feelings; these feelings, in turn, translate into actions. Repeated actions form habits, good or bad—virtues or vices. Consequently, the sum of these actions terminates in our destiny: salvation or damnation, heaven or hell.

Do you want to keep custody of your eyes and thereby persevere in holiness? Here are five ways to help you use your eyes properly so that you can indeed live out that challenging beatitude of Jesus: "Blessed are the pure in heart, for they shall see God."

Pray to St. Lucy and St. Raphael.

There are two patron saints of the eyes whom you can invoke: St. Lucy, a virgin martyr of the early Church, and the archangel Raphael, who is one of the key figures in the book of Tobit (through Raphael's powerful intercession, Tobit's sight was completely restored). Call on these powerful allies, who contemplate the beatific vision of God, to help you use your eyes to behold what is beautiful, true, and good in this life so as to contemplate God's face for all eternity.

Contemplate Images.

One of the rich treasures of Catholicism is the honoring and venerating of images—statues and paintings of Jesus, Mary, and saints and angels. I highly recommend that you enthrone in your home attractive pictures of Jesus, Mary, and the saints. Seek out an image of Our Lady of Guadalupe, for instance, or of Our Lady of Fátima, or of the Divine Mercy or the Sacred Heart of Jesus. Seeing such images placed prominently throughout your home will encourage you to be pure.

Contemplate the Eyes of Jesus.

St. Ignatius of Loyola suggests that we start our contemplation by placing ourselves in the presence of God and then imagining "the loving gaze of God" upon us. The Gospel often presents Jesus gazing, peering, and looking into the eyes of others, with profound effects. Jesus' loving and merciful gaze into the eyes of Simon Peter after he had betrayed the Lord elicited tears of deep contrition and repentance (see Luke 22:61–62). The eyes of Jesus, seeing St. Matthew, moved the future evangelist to leave all to follow his Lord (see Matt. 9:9).

As he hung on the Cross between the two thieves, Jesus looked to the repentant thief and obtained a last-minute conversion (see Luke 23:42–43). Of course, one of the best ways to contemplate the eyes of Jesus is to gaze at the Blessed Sacrament—the body, blood, soul, and divinity of Jesus. His eyes also are present in the Blessed Sacrament. As the psalmist writes: "Look to him, and be radiant" (Ps. 34:5).

See God's Beauty in Nature.
What element in nature most appeals to you as a bridge to elevate you to the beauty of the Creator? The beauty of creation is merely a pale glimpse of the utter beauty of the Creator, God himself. God indeed is wisdom, love, and beauty.

Read the Word of God.
A proper use of our eyes is the reading of the word of God, that lamp for our steps and light for our path (cf. Ps. 119:105). Steve Wood, in his excellent booklet *Breaking Free: 12 Steps to Sexual Purity for Men*, states:

> One of the few effective means of getting these pornographic images out of your mind is spending time reading and memorizing Scripture every day. For many of you it might be particularly helpful if you have a Scripture time both morning and evening. In addition, you need to begin

a program of memorizing Scripture. In my experience, a disciplined plan to memorize Scripture is necessary to clear the rot out of your brain. "Occupy your minds with good thoughts, or the enemy will fill them with bad ones. Unoccupied, they cannot be" (St. Thomas More).[21]

As an analogy, consider how chlorine kills the bacteria in a swimming pool — *that* is what scripture, God's powerful word, does to kill the rot of bad images engraved on our memories.

Let us end with a quote from St. John Berchmans, a Jesuit who died in his early twenties: "I desire to keep my eyes pure in this life so as to contemplate the majestic beauty of the face of Mary for all eternity."[22] Inspired by his dedication, let us make a pact with our eyes to contemplate only that which is pure, noble, edifying, and innocent so as to live out to the fullest possible extent Jesus' challenge: "Blessed are the pure in heart, for they shall see God."

[21] Steve Wood, *Breaking Free: 12 Steps to Sexual Purity for Men* (Greenville: Family Life Center Publications, 2003), 5.
[22] Secastiano Berettari, *The Lives of Joseph Anchieta, Alvera Van Virmundt, and John Berchmans* (Cambridge: Cambridge University Press, 2011), 408.

11

Cultivate Gratitude

Do you suffer from that common malady known as "complaini-tus"? The symptoms include complaining and grumbling at a constant rate throughout the day — about the weather, co-workers, difficult situations, family problems, health issues, and so on.

If we find reasons to complain about anybody, anything, and any circumstance, may God grant us a true conversion of heart. If we are disciples of Jesus, we should fight vigorously against negativism and that infirmity known as "complainitus."

Shakespeare expressed it forcefully: "How sharper than a ser-pent's tooth it is to have a thankless child!"[23] Another quotation that comes to mind is also apropos to the topic: "I complained because I had no shoes until I met somebody without any feet." Jesus was amazed that after he had healed ten lepers of their ter-rible and incurable disease, only one of them returned to give thanks (see Luke 17:11–19).

Let us therefore fight against "complainitus" by cultivating an attitude of gratitude. The reasons for being grateful are countless, but here are five that you might have forgotten about:

[23] William Shakespeare, *King Lear*, act 1, scene 4.

Life

Thank the generous Lord for having given you natural life and, even more, *supernatural life* and union with God through the sacrament of Baptism. Through Baptism you became a child of God the Father, a brother or sister of Jesus the Lord, and an intimate friend of the Holy Spirit. Lord, I praise you and thank you.

The Eucharist

The word *Eucharist* from Greek means "thanksgiving." How exceedingly grateful we should be for the real presence of Jesus in the Blessed Sacrament—during Mass, in Holy Communion, and always present for us to visit in the tabernacle. "Come to me, all who labor and are heavy laden, and I will give you rest" (Matt. 11:28).

Mercy

"Give thanks to the Lord, for he is good, for his mercy endures forever" (Dan. 3:67). In a cutthroat world in which mercy is quickly evaporating from the modern scene, we know and believe that our God is a merciful God. As the psalmist emphasizes: "Our God is slow to anger and rich in mercy" (cf. Ps. 145:8). Even though we might fall, we know that the arms of the Father are always wide open to receive us as soon as we say, "Jesus, mercy."

The Holy Spirit

Many are the sublime names for the Holy Spirit: Sanctifier, Counselor, Consoler, Advocate, Paraclete, Gift of Gifts, Breath of God, Love between Father and Son, Finger of God, and Sweet Guest of the Soul. By maintaining the state of sanctifying grace in your soul, you can enjoy, at any time, this Sweet Guest and the consolation he brings.

Mary, Our Mother

Recall the story of St. Juan Diego and his dying uncle. On his way to fetch a priest, he was stopped by Our Lady of Guadalupe, who dispelled his fears and anxieties with these words: "Do not be afraid. Am I not your mother? I have you in the crossing of my arms." Rejoice and give thanks to God for the great gift of Mary. Remember always, but especially in moments of trial, that Mary is your Mother and has you in the crossing of her arms. She has you hidden in the inner recesses of her most pure and Immaculate Heart.

Find something to be thankful for. Although you might be frustrated by the storms of life, there are ways that you can begin to feel thanksgiving in your heart, no matter what your situation. Think of holy Job when he heard of all the terrible calamities that befell him. His sons were dead, his fortune stolen, and his life seemed to come to chaos, yet he fell to the ground and proclaimed, "The Lord gave, and the Lord hath taken away: as it hath pleased the Lord so is it done: blessed be the name of the Lord" (Job 1:21, Douay-Rheims). Even in his greatest agony, Job still praised God.

Like Job, seek to cultivate gratitude and praise, even when the storms of life are heavy. When you want to complain, instead think of five things you are thankful for. No matter what, you will find something to thank God for today. Look to the list above and then find a few more things, even if they are small things such as sleep, food, or shelter. These are things that many in the world go without, and you should feel intense gratitude for them.

If you can do nothing else, give thanks to God that he is there and hears you. In the book of Jeremiah, our Lord declares, "For

I know the plans I have for you, says the LORD, plans for welfare and not for evil, to give you a future and a hope" (Jer. 29:11). If he created you, he thinks of you and is there to hear you. What a great friend and advocate he is.

12

Build Up with Words

You can probably remember having been hurt by somebody who, perhaps without thinking, said something that stung your heart and left a lasting bad memory. You have also likely opened your mouth without sufficient reflection and, as a result, wounded a brother, a sister, or a friend. Immediately after the word slipped out of your mouth, you wanted to reel it back in, but it was too late. Once the word has been uttered, there is no "muting," cancelling, or postponing its arrival at the ear and heart of the listener.

Jesus speaks very clearly about our words: "I tell you, on the day of judgment men will render account for every careless word they utter" (Matt. 12:36). St. James dedicates almost the entire third chapter of his letter to sins of the tongue. In short, the apostle underscores the importance of learning the art of speech, reminding us that we should be slow to speak and quick to listen. He reminds us that man can control almost all types of animals, but not the tongue. Moreover, he says that the same tongue that is used to praise God ends up cursing one's neighbor. This is wrong.

So here are a few suggestions to help you use your tongue, speech, words, and conversations to edify and build up your neighbor:

Talk to God First and Then to Your Neighbor.

It was said of the great St. Dominic, founder of the Order of Preachers (among which were St. Albert the Great and his student St. Thomas Aquinas), that he would first talk to God and then talk about God to others. Ideally that should be our motto and objective in life with regard to speech — that our words in some way communicate the presence of God to others.

Think Before You Speak.

St. Ignatius, in numbers 313 through 336 of his *Spiritual Exercises*, explains how our interior actions are moved by good spirits and evil spirits according to our individual spiritual situations. He observes that an agitated soul is in a state of desolation and will thus speak ill to people around him; in this state, it is not the good spirit that is guiding him but the bad.

Speak after reflection and with a calm and peaceful mind. Examine and contemplate your thoughts before speaking to people around you. Rushed and impetuous words from unclear or muddled ideas often cause confusion and hurt. Avoid them.

Practice Silence.

Pope Benedict XVI insisted on the importance of cultivating silence in our daily lives. Most of us suffer from noise pollution: radio talk shows, pop music, around-the-clock TV programs, nonstop chatter and gossip. Pope Benedict went so far as to say that if we do not have zones of silence, we really cannot understand the people who want to talk to us.

Silence creates an interior space for listening; listening disposes us to union with the Holy Spirit; the Holy Spirit teaches us to pray and then to listen attentively and charitably to our brothers and sisters.

Follow the Golden Rule in Your Speech.

The golden rule enunciated by Jesus is very simple: "[A]s you wish that men would do to you, *do so to them*" (Luke 6:31, emphasis added). Apply the golden rule to your speech. That is to say, "As you wish that men would speak to you, *speak so to them*."

At times it is not clear if what we are saying is harmful to others or beneficial. What can be of great help in this matter is to imagine Jesus, Mary, and St. Joseph present during your conversation, observing your choice of words, your tone of voice, and even your facial expressions, and to consider whether they would be nodding and smiling with approval. This is the acid test for followers of Jesus. Are our words pleasing in the sight of God, his holy Mother, and good St. Joseph (who never said a word in all of Sacred Scripture)?

In her *Diary*, St. Faustina confessed that one of her three primary faults was talking too much. She admitted that Jesus had revealed to her that at times he preferred her to be silent rather than to speak, and for two reasons: her would-be listener would not profit from her words, and it would be much more beneficial for the souls in purgatory to have her prayers (in those moments) rather than her conversation. This is very helpful to remember.

St. Bonaventure tells us that we should open our mouths on three occasions: to praise God, to accuse ourselves, and to edify our neighbor. Faithful to this exhortation, we will surely avoid many slips of the tongue; anoint our words with the Spirit, and store up for ourselves an eternal inheritance in heaven.

May our Lady, who pondered things in her Immaculate Heart before speaking, teach us to magnify the Lord in our words and to edify our neighbor. *My soul magnifies the Lord, and my spirit rejoices in God my Savior* (Luke 1:46–47).

13

Bring the Bible into Your Life

Pope Benedict XVI encouraged us to deepen our prayer life in the classical method of Lectio Divina (divine reading), through which we read the Bible as an aid to our prayer lives. Let us here explore the steps that the Holy Father suggested:

Lectio

Choose a text to meditate on. Invite the Holy Spirit, the Interior Master, to help you in prayer. You can use the prayer of the young Samuel: "Speak, LORD, for thy servant hears" (1 Sam. 3:9). What a privilege you have — that God wants to speak to your heart. Read the text you have chosen.

Meditatio

After you have read your chosen passage, pause and consider what you have read. Go over every word as if it were the first time you've read it. Now apply the use of your memory and understanding to discover what God is saying to you through the text you have read. Rejoice in the fact that God has a special message he wants to communicate to you through this reading and meditation. Pray: "Lord God, what is the message you want to communicate to my heart right now?" Sit quietly and listen with your heart for the Holy Spirit's response.

Contemplatio

Now use another mental faculty with which God has endowed you: your imagination. We all have an imagination — maybe even a very vivid one. You can use your imagination to reconstruct the place, time, and surroundings of what you read. Maybe you read the Sermon on the Mount, and you can use the eye of your mind to see Jesus on that mount; use the ears of your mind to hear his words and even your other senses to imagine the smells, the tastes, and the feelings Jesus' listeners experienced as those words fell from his lips. It is a great gift of God that we can see and experience his word in our minds and hearts.

The imagination, however, is like a two-edged sword: it can be used for good or for evil. A married man, for instance, could use his imagination for evil by daydreaming about a past girlfriend, thereby committing adultery of the heart. A better use of the imagination is to picture yourself walking side by side with the Good Shepherd (see Ps. 23; John 10:1–18), contemplating his loving gaze peering into your eyes, hearing his gentle and reassuring voice, and experiencing his strong but loving embrace. However we use our imagination, it must be trained for the pursuit of good.

Oracio

Now we have arrived at the very heart of the essence and purpose of Lectio Divina and of prayer itself, *oracio* meaning "prayer." When your mind or your imagination sparks an idea or an image from your meditative readings, it is time to descend into your heart and open up in prayer. This means to open your heart and talk to the Lord in the most simple, trusting, and intimate way. Let the Lord use this image from your readings to teach you and to awaken you to further lessons on how best to imitate Jesus. Keep going over this idea in your heart, inquiring what this could mean for you.

Accio

Authentic prayer must be brought into the reality of our lives. In *accio*, we bring action to what we have contemplated. The Doctor of Prayer, St. Teresa of Ávila, astutely observed that authentic prayer manifests itself by how it affects our lives. Does our deep prayer lead us to live holier lives and to follow in the steps of Jesus? Jesus reminds us that we can tell a tree by its fruits: a good tree will bring forth good fruit, and a bad tree will bring forth bad fruit (see Matt. 7:17). Praying with sincerity, honesty, rectitude of intention, and love for God will bring forth fruits or virtues in our lives.

Our Lady is our example: in the Annunciation, we contemplate Mary in prayer as a contemplative. After she finishes her prayer, "[L]et it be to me according to your word" (Luke 1:38), she hurries to bring the fruits of her prayer in service to her cousin Elizabeth. May our Lady's example motivate us to be "contemplatives in action."

Transformacio

Our Lectio Divina should bring about a gradual *transformation* in our daily lives. Our aim should be to implement the words of the great apostle St. Paul: "[I]t is no longer I who live, but Christ who lives in me" (Gal. 2:20). This is the ultimate goal of Lectio Divina and of all authentic prayer—the imitation of Jesus Christ, the following in his footsteps, and transformation in him.

Lectio Divina can truly deepen your prayer life. Choose your text, read it, meditate, contemplate, and pray — and then live it out and allow God, through the working of the Holy Spirit, to transform you into the saint he has made you to be.

14

Spiritual Warfare

Our life on earth is a battle—not against one another, but against evil. Through the sacrament of Confirmation, we receive the gifts of the Holy Spirit—wisdom, understanding, counsel, knowledge, fortitude, piety, and fear of the Lord—and are transformed into soldiers of Christ the King. With the Cristero martyrs of Mexico, our battle cry must be "Viva Cristo Rey!" *Long live Christ the King!*

The devil has keen intelligence (although he uses it in a perverted way). He is exceedingly sly and crafty and constantly at work. Fortunately, God, Mary, and the holy angels and saints are far more powerful than the devil.

Two extremes must be avoided with respect to the devil. These were warnings given by Blessed Pope Paul VI. The first extreme is to deny that the devil exists. Indeed, convincing souls that he doesn't exist is one of the most effective tactics of the devil. On the other hand, we should never give the devil too much importance. Fearful alarmists speak more of the power of the devil than of the omnipotence of God. Let us avoid these extremes.

Here are some tactics you can use in your spiritual battles:

Be Vigilant in Prayer.

"Watch and pray" (Matt. 26:41) so that you will not be put to the test and be overcome by the temptations of the devil. The reason for the apostles' abandoning Jesus in the Garden of Gethsemane was that they were not vigilant in prayer.

Name It and Claim It.

When a temptation arises, it can prove exceedingly useful simply to admit in a very calm manner, "I am being tempted by the devil, the enemy of God." Name it, claim it, and then tame it. Discovering the enemy on the attack is half the battle. Ignorance of the enemy's presence can augment his power over us.

Avoid the Near Occasion of Sin.

Often we are tempted because we do not avoid near occasions of sin. Do not play with fire. One of the reasons Eve ate the forbidden fruit was because she was near the tree whose fruit God had told her not to eat.

Escape the State of Desolation.

For the times when we find ourselves in a state of desolation, St. Ignatius arms us with four weapons: more prayer, more meditation, an examination of conscience (to see why you are in desolation), and some suitable penance. Some devils are expelled only through prayer and penance (see Mark 9:29).

Use Sacramentals.

Sacramentals are "sacred signs which bear a resemblance to the sacraments. They signify effects, particularly of a spiritual nature, which are obtained through the intercession of the Church. By them men are disposed to receive the chief effect of the sacraments, and various occasions in life are rendered holy" (*Catechism of the Catholic Church*, no. 1667). A sacramental can be an article (such as a crucifix or a medal), an action (such as blessing yourself with holy water), or a blessing (such as the blessing of candles or of meals). The proper use of sacramentals can prove to be very efficacious in fighting against the devil, and especially these three: the scapular of Our Lady of Mount Carmel, the medal of St. Benedict, and holy water. St. Teresa of Ávila insisted on using holy water to expel the devil. Why? The devil is inflated with pride, and holy water is small and inconspicuous; the devil hates this and cannot endure it.

Offer Short, Fervent Prayers.

When being assaulted by the enemy, it is imperative that you offer short, fervent prayers. These can be very effective in putting the devil to flight. Here are some examples of these powerful prayers:

Jesus, I trust in you.
Sweet heart of Mary, be my salvation.
Lord, save me.
Lord, come to my rescue.

And, of course, it is always helpful to invoke with faith and confidence the holy names of Jesus, Mary, and St. Joseph.

Reject Temptation Immediately.

A danger in spiritual combat is our lethargic and anemic response to temptation. God's grace must always prevail through the weapon of prayer. Still, we must engage our will in virtuously and forcefully rejecting temptations from the start. Frequently temptations get a stronghold over us because we open the door and the tail of the devil enters, and it is difficult to kick him out.

Avoid Laziness.

The *Diary* of St. Faustina mentions an occasion in which the devil was roaming the corridors, frantically looking for somebody to tempt. St. Faustina stopped the devil and commanded him to tell her, out of obedience to Jesus, what was the most effective tool for conquering the nuns. Reluctantly the devil responded: lazy and indolent souls.

The great St. John Bosco mortally feared vacation time for his boys in the Oratory. Why? Too much free time gives full entrance and game to the devil in the life of the youth. How often our sins are preceded by moments, hours, or even days of laziness. St. John Bosco (1815–1888) said, "We will rest in heaven."[24] Now it is time to work out our salvation in fear and trembling (cf. Phil. 2:12). May St. Benedict's motto be ours: *Ora et labora*—Pray and work.

Follow the Three Examples of Jesus in the Desert (Matt. 4:1–11).

Of course, our best example is Jesus, who said, "I am the way, and the truth, and the life" (John 14:6). After Jesus had spent forty days in the desert, the devil tempted him. Jesus forcefully and easily conquered him by using three weapons: prayer, fasting, and the word of God. Jesus had a prolonged prayer experience in the desert. Added to that was forty days of fasting. Finally, when the devil tempted him by using the word of God, Jesus responded by using the word of God himself and thus resisted Satan's efforts.

[24] F. A. Forbes, *Saint John Bosco: The Friend of Youth* (Rockford, IL: TAN Books, 1962), chap. 8.

Fervent and prolonged prayer, constant self-denial, and familiarity with the word of God—both meditating on it and putting it into practice—are efficacious weapons to combat and conquer Satan.

Be Open to Your Spiritual Director.

Recall from chapter 4 that in the thirteenth rule for discernment of the *Spiritual Exercises*, St. Ignatius warns us that the devil likes *secrecy*; therefore, if you are in a profound state of desolation, opening up to a spiritual director can help you conquer temptation. Just as you would reveal a wound to a doctor, so should you reveal the wounds of your soul to an able spiritual director.

Overwhelmed by temptation, doubt, and confusion shortly before making her vows, St. Thérèse opened up to her novice mistress and superior and revealed her state of soul. Almost immediately, her temptation disappeared, and she made her vows and went on to be one of the greatest modern saints. What would have happened to her if, following the counsel of the devil, she had kept her state of soul secret?

Call on St. Michael the Archangel.

In our battle with Satan, we should use all the weapons in our arsenal. God chose St. Michael the Archangel, the prince of the heavenly host, to cast into hell Satan and the other rebellious angels. St. Michael, whose name means, "Who is like unto God?", is still as powerful. In the midst of the storm of temptations, call on St. Michael. You can pray the famous prayer, "St. Michael the Archangel, defend us in battle ..." or simply beg for his intercession. His help from the heights of heaven will help you win your combat with the devil.

Turn to Mary Most Holy.

The Mexican people have great devotion to Mary, especially under the title of Our Lady of Guadalupe. In Guadalajara, Mexico, however, in addition to venerating Mary, Our Lady of Guadalupe, as patron of Mexico and the Americas, they honor her with another title: *La General del ejercito* (General of the army). In our battle against the ancient serpent, Genesis 3:15 honors the woman who crushes the head of the serpent: "I will put enmity between you and the woman and between your seed and her seed; he shall bruise your head, and you shall bruise his heel" (Gen. 3:15). Indeed, the ancient serpent, the devil, can strike at us, but if we rely on and trust in Mary, she will crush his ugly head.

Turn to Mary by offering three Hail Marys each morning as you begin your day and then three more before you go to bed in thanksgiving for her help in your daily battles. While you drive to work, offer a decade of the Rosary for guidance and protection. Our Mother is always there for you and cares enough about you to offer her assistance and to intercede for you with her son, our Lord Jesus Christ.

15

Fight for the Family

Divorce rates have skyrocketed to an all-time high. Adultery is rampant. So-called trial marriages result in separation and the abandonment of children to one-parent families. The homosexual agenda promotes same-sex "marriage," including the adopting of children, and calls it the "modern family." Pornography invades homes — more precisely, it is *invited in* — producing powerful addictions that lead people to total alienation from members of their family.

This is a bird's-eye view of the family situation in the modern world. Nonetheless, followers of Jesus Christ lift the banner with the word *hope*.

Hope is one of the theological virtues (along with faith and charity) that are infused into our soul at Baptism. It is the virtue by which we place our total trust in God. Despite our failures, weaknesses, shortcomings, sins, and total fragility, we know that God is our rock, our fortress, and our light in the midst of darkness. As the archangel Gabriel announced to Mary: "For with God nothing will be impossible" (Luke 1:37).

With that in mind I would like to emphasize the importance of fathers in the formation of wholesome, solid, and holy families. The mother is the heart of the family, but the father is the head.

What, then, are the *goals* that every married man should aim for so that he can live out what is true fatherhood in a world of drop-out dads, negligent fathers, and overly timid men?

Reflect God the Father.

To be a good *father* he should first be a good *son of God the Father*, whom he represents and reflects. If a father has a spiritual identity crisis — that is to say, if he does not understand his intimate relationship with God the Father — he will not be able to transmit to his children an authentic vision of God the Father. If, however, he has encountered God the Father in an intimate, personal, filial, and convincing way, he will be able to transmit this fatherhood to those whom God has placed in his care.

A prime example can be found in the life of Karol Wojtyla, who would become Pope John Paul II. He lost his mother at age nine and his older brother three years later, leaving him with only his father. Karol recalled waking up before dawn and seeing the figure of his father kneeling, deeply absorbed in prayer. This example of his father left an indelible impression on the young Karol. His father had a deep and intimate relationship with God the Father and transmitted this to his son. This was an undeniably important factor in the development of the man who would someday become Pope John Paul II, one of the greatest and clearest reflections of true fatherhood in the history of the world.

Love Your Wife.

After placing primary emphasis on his relationship with God the Father, a true father should *love his wife*. The love and friendship that he has with his wife should be indispensable. This love should not stagnate or, worse, fizzle out. On the contrary, this human love, blessed supernaturally by the sacrament of holy Matrimony, should blossom, grow, and flourish until the moment of death.

All too many marriages lose their vibrancy; the spouses' love grows cold to the point that both live in the same house as if they were strangers to each other, and the children suffer the consequences. How can spouses keep the flame enkindled and burning bright? Both husband and wife should cultivate an ever-deepening relationship with God. This should include prayer (both individually and as a family), the sacraments (frequent Confession and Holy Communion), and devotion to Mary, particularly through the daily recitation of the holy rosary. All of these help to form a relationship with God and foster unity between husband and wife.

Love Your Children.

The father should love his children and see himself as the ladder by which they can climb to heaven. In other words, an authentic father should first provide for the *spiritual needs* of his children. He should teach his young children to pray. Little children absorb what they are taught like sponges. As sponges can absorb dirty water or clean water, children can absorb the dirt of the modern world or, through the help of a good father, what is pure, noble, and uplifting.

The father should teach his children, *especially* prayer. Men can sometimes be sheepish when it comes to praying publicly. They shouldn't be. Remember Moses, bravely keeping his arms elevated so that his people could win the battle (Exod. 17:8–13). In the same way, a father must keep his arms open to the Lord, asking for strength and guidance, and *let his family see him doing it.*

Until we have restored the essential role of the father in the family to its proper place, *the world will suffer intensely*. The man who is called to the vocation of marriage assumes an enormously important responsibility. The goal of the vocation is holiness of life and a heavenly reward.

Let us turn to the best of earthly fathers, St. Joseph, and beg for his powerful intercession. *St. Joseph, patron of families, patron of fathers, pray for us!*

16

A Jonah Complex

Jonah is considered a minor prophet, and his book in the Bible is relatively short, but it has an explosive message.

God summoned Jonah to go to a place where he did not want to go, to give a message to a people he detested — the pagan Ninevites.

Jonah's response to God's call was a flat and unequivocal no. To prove it, Jonah jumped into a pagan ship going in the opposite direction. He reasoned that this would free him from this task.

God had other plans. When God wants to carry out a mission, he finds the wherewithal to accomplish it. God sent two unexpected surprises to Jonah: a powerful storm and a huge fish. The sudden storm compelled the sailors of the pagan ship to question who provoked it by angering the gods. Jonah pleaded guilty and told the sailors to cast him into the sea. When they had no other choice, the sailors did as Jonah had asked, and immediately the storm ceased. Jonah was swallowed by a huge fish, in whose belly he remained for three long days and nights. Then the fish spewed Jonah out of its mouth, and he ended up in the very place he had tried to avoid — the huge city of Nineveh. When God wants something done, he sometimes carries it out in surprising ways.

So Jonah, the resistant prophet of the Lord, started out on his mission of preaching to the enormous, sinful, pagan-filled city of Nineveh. His message, clear and to the point, was one of conversion or condemnation: "In forty days Nineveh and its entire people will be destroyed!" (cf. Jon. 3:4). The message of doom reached the ears of the king, and the result was shocking: a total call to conversion for the whole kingdom, nobody excluded, not even the animals. Men and women, young and old, even the four-footed creatures had imposed on them both a rigorous fast and an outward display of penance—the donning of sackcloth and ashes. Peering down from heaven upon the humbled and repentant Ninevites, God pointed out to Jonah their attitude of conversion, their change of heart. Consequently, God himself decides not to chastise the Ninevites.

Jonah becomes irritated at God's decision. He had been expecting another Sodom and Gomorrah event to be displayed at Nineveh. He wanted revenge and justice to be leveled on the city, but God is slow to anger and rich in mercy. Man, on the contrary, is quick to anger and slow to forgiveness. God's thoughts are not our thoughts; as high as the heavens are above the earth, so are God's thoughts above ours (cf. Isa. 55:8–9).

In how many ways are you able to identify with the person of Jonah? Do you suffer from a "Jonah complex"? How often have you heard God call you clearly—as in the case of Jonah—and yet purposely closed your ears to that call or even turned your back on God? And how often has God, in his divine providence and infinite goodness, sought you out despite your resistance and flight from him, pursuing you and tracking you down?

Sometimes God intervenes by sending a powerful storm—spiritual, emotional, moral, social, familial, or economic—into our lives to bring us back to the right path. God is a mortal enemy of complacency. In a clear and cutting way, God reminds us of this in the book of Revelation: "[Y]ou are neither cold nor hot. Would that you were cold or hot! So, because you are lukewarm, and neither cold nor hot, I will spew you out of my mouth" (Rev. 3:15–16).

Sometimes God is forced to descend in torments, storms, and tempests to shock us out of our lukewarm, anemic, indolent spiritual malaise. St. Augustine reacted violently to lukewarmness — after God had sent storms into his life — with these words: "Thou breathedst odours, and I drew in breath and panted for Thee. I tasted, and hunger and thirst. Thou touchedst me, and I burned for Thy peace."[25] When God shocks us, he is looking for our obedience so that he might work good in the world through us.

Consider the good that can be accomplished when you cooperate with God's plan. God wanted to use Jonah as his instrument, and when Jonah finally cooperated, an entire city converted. Could it be that God is calling you to be a Jonah? Could your timidity, your fear, your lack of trust in God be blocking his work through you — work that could lead to the salvation of souls? Today if you hear His voice, harden not your heart (cf. Ps. 95:7–8).

[25] St. Augustine, *The Confessions of St. Augustine*, trans. E. B. Pusey (New York, E. P. Dutton, 1900), 259.

17

The Two Worst Things in the Universe

If you stepped on a rusty nail, you would extract the nail and go to the doctor for a tetanus shot. If your little daughter accidentally drank poison, you would call the paramedics and rush her to the hospital. Surely you would not go a week without showering. You would even remove instantaneously something as simple as a dirt particle in your eye.

We are keenly aware of our bodily needs, especially in times of suffering or sickness. What about our souls?

How many commit mortal sin (or many mortal sins) and do nothing to remove this mortal spiritual sickness? Mortal sin kills the life of grace in our soul. Pope John Paul II called it moral suicide.

The two worst things that could befall us would be to commit a mortal sin and subsequently die in the *state* of mortal sin. If this happened, we would lose our immortal soul for all eternity.

Those who commit mortal sins and purposely postpone repentance, conversion, and Confession are, in fact, committing another sin—the sin of *presumption*. Presumption means that we presume on God's grace; we believe that he is so loving and kind and patient that he will always give us many more chances and

will wait for us forever. This is a dangerous and sinful presumption to make, and it will put us in danger.

We know neither the day nor the hour when the Lord will
knock at the door of our hearts and ask us for a reckoning of our
lives. He will come to judge the living and the dead. He will
come like a thief in the night; at the hour that we least expect
(see Matt. 24:42–43).

If you are in a state of mortal sin, do not put off your conversion but immediately turn to the Lord, repent, trust in his infinite
mercy, confess your sins, return to the state of grace, and strive
with all your energy to be faithful to the Lord and to guard your
soul against its three enemies: the world, the flesh, and the devil.

Begin regularly to seek out a priest for Confession. If St. John
Paul II could find a reason to go to Confession weekly, you should
be able to go regularly. Start by searching your life and reading
the Ten Commandments and see where you might have fallen
short of the ideal. Then seek out your priest to make a sincere
confession with contrition of heart. Do right away the penance
your confessor gives you, and if he offers you any advice, act on it.

If you make this movement of your heart a regular habit, you
will find areas in your life where you can continue to improve
and draw closer to Jesus. In this fight of your life, the grace of
God will be in your corner, and you will be sure to live a happy
life and thus have an even happier life after death.

Let us turn to Mary, Mother of Mercy, to help us fight against
sin, to treasure living in the state of grace, and to hope in heaven.
Mary, Mother of God, pray for us!

18

Root Out Envy

Sibling rivalry; anger over someone else hit the game-winning homerun; depression over the beauty that her best friend has and she does not; disappointment that his small car and his shotgun apartment don't compare to his old classmate's Jaguar and multimillion-dollar house with a swimming pool—these are all signs of envy.

Envy is one of the capital sins; the *Catechism of the Catholic Church* defines it as "sadness at the sight of another's goods and the immoderate desire to acquire them for oneself, even unjustly" and adds, "When it wishes grave harm to a neighbor it is a mortal sin" (no. 2539). It is an ugly sin that frustrates the greatest of virtues—fraternal charity, which means loving and wishing good to our neighbor.

In many places in the Old and the New Testaments, the ugly serpent of envy raises its head, leading to lethal consequences when not subdued and conquered. For instance, we read in Genesis the account of the sons of Adam and Eve, the brothers Cain and Abel. Seeing that God preferred Abel's offering to his, Cain was envious. Filled with bitter hatred, he led his brother to a field and killed him (Gen. 4:3–8). This is the result of envy left unchecked—murder, even of one's own brother.

Later in scripture, King Saul becomes obsessed with David's superiority over him and attempts (but fails) to kill him. His drive to be better than David even leads him to betray God himself, by abandoning trust in the Almighty and seeking the aid of the witch of Endor. Ironically, Saul asks the witch to summon the dead prophet Samuel, who predicts defeat for Saul—because the Lord had departed from the king due to his envy. In the end, in the midst of a losing battle, the desperate, tragic Saul ends his life by falling on his sword (1 Sam. 28:5–19; 31:1–4).

The most serious manifestation of the evil of envy is in the death of Jesus. Although born in Bethlehem; brought up and raised in Nazareth, a very inconspicuous town—"Can anything good come out of Nazareth?" (John 1:46)—the son of a humble carpenter, Jesus spoke with eloquence and power and miraculously healed countless people. Many of the Pharisees and teachers of the law could not accept somebody who was so unknown and uneducated yet made such a powerful impression on the people. Therefore, they taunted him, attacked him, derided him, tried to contradict him, and finally had him crucified. One of the principal reasons behind the Crucifixion and death of Jesus was envy.

Giving in to the capital sin of envy can wreak havoc in your soul. As soon as you are aware of a temptation to envy, it is incumbent upon you to reject it. If you don't, these are some of the ugly consequences:

- *Anxiety of soul.* Envy can lead you to compare yourself obsessively with everyone you meet. This robs your soul of peace.

- *Gossip and slander.* Envy often spills over into bitter and damaging words—as simple as gossip or as serious as slander or calumny. Jesus says, "Out of the abundance of the heart the mouth speaks" (Matt. 12:34). Envy is a sign of a sick heart, and ugly words manifest it.

* *Insomnia.* The envious person often cannot sleep at night because he is so worried about the progress and success of his "rival." This leads to even more sin as the envious person becomes irate, impatient, pushy, overly demanding, harsh, and bitter toward others — all as a result of sleepless nights brought on by envy.

* *Ulcers.* Sin is our worse enemy. It actually leads to physical ailments, such as the formation of ulcers.

* *Family fights.* Sibling rivalry brought on by envy leads to quarrels, fights, and suspicions, depriving a family of the harmony and peace that are so necessary for wholesome family life.

* *Sabotage.* An envious person can become bent on seeing the downfall of his supposed rival — as we saw with Cain and Abel, with David and Saul, and against Jesus. The envious person can look for opportunities to put stumbling blocks in the way of his rival to destroy him, but really he is destroying himself. Even if he does not actively seek to bring ruin to his rival, he may take delight in his falls and weaknesses and may seek to humiliate him.

* *Murder.* Envy is like a snowball rolling down a mountain: the momentum can increase the snowball to a huge size. Envy leads to resentment, resentment leads to hatred, and hatred can culminate in murder if fully

mature. Don't forget what happened to Cain and King Saul. It is not always the case that envy will lead to murder, but the hate that an envious person can have in his heart can ruin his soul.

- *Destruction of charity.* Envy can lead to wishing evil and failure on another; whereas charity desires the good of others. Charity is the greatest of virtues, and we shall be judged on it at the end of our life, as St. John of the Cross so clearly expresses: "At the evening of life, we shall be judged on our love."[26]

- *Frustration of spiritual progress.* The Mystical Doctor, St. John of the Cross, explains that there are two aspects of envy: physical (material) and spiritual. Spiritual envy manifests itself often in the person who sincerely pursues a life of great spiritual depth. Instead of focusing on God, however, he is always observing and comparing himself to his "spiritual rival," hoping that his rival will pray less, diminish the intensity of his spiritual program, and fall behind in the pursuit of holiness. How contrary to charity is spiritual envy, and how displeasing to Jesus, whose commandment was, "[L]ove one another as I have loved you" (John 15:12).

Don't let envy fester inside you. Examine your life, your actions, and, most importantly, your *intentions.* Instead of being envious of what others have, take time to thank God that he has blessed your brother or your sister in Christ with such great gifts

[26] Geoffrey Chapman, trans., *Catechism of the Catholic Church* (London: Burns and Oates, 1994), 233

and recognize how he has blessed you. There are different gifts and blessings for different people at various times, and you surely are blessed as a child of God. Instead of dwelling on the gifts of others, see what you have to be joyful about in your own life.

When your mind dwells on envy, recognize that thought, and turn it to the good in your own life. Then ask for mercy and forgiveness for having such envy, and ask God to soften your heart toward those toward whom you envy. Learn the Thomistic prayer that asks "that I may never envy my neighbor's possessions and ever give thanks for your good things."[27]

Through adequate spiritual direction and Confession, light can shine in our souls to see this interior wound of envy, and then Jesus the divine physician can touch these wounds and heal them.

[27] St. Thomas Aquinas, *The Aquinas Prayer Book*, trans. Robert Anderson and Johann Moser (Manchester, NH: Sophia Institute Press, 2000), 35.

19

How to Beat Greed

Psychologist Erich Fromm coined this immortal maxim: "If you are what you have and you lose what you have, who are you?" We tend to equate the value of our lives with the amount of money we have and with the possessions that money buys us, which is why the Bible warns us that love of money is the root of all evil. Or, as the Beatles put it, "Money can't buy me love."

Greed is one of the seven capital sins. The capital sins can be divided into two categories: (1) those that refer more to the corporal nature — gluttony, lust, greed, and sloth; and (2) those that refer more to the spiritual and intellectual nature — anger, envy, and pride.

Being sons and daughters of Adam and Eve, we have all inherited original sin, and therefore we all carry in our nature bad tendencies to commit capital sins. If these tendencies are not held in check, they will become actual sins. If they are allowed to multiply, they can become vices, which results in slavery to sin.

Let us now define the capital sin of greed and examine practical steps to overcome it, for there is no doubt that this deadly interior attitude must be overcome in order to attain a fully developed Christian life.

Greed is the disordered desire for material things. Notice the importance of the qualifier—*disordered*. The book of Genesis constantly reminds us that all of creation is good. The evil is to be found not in the reality of creation but in the human heart's disordered desire for it.

In the Gospel, a rich young man who knew the Ten Commandments approached Jesus and asked him the way to eternal life. Jesus told him to obey the Ten Commandments; this he proudly claimed he had done. Then Jesus looked at him with love and challenged him: "If you would be perfect, go, sell what you possess and give to the poor, and you will have treasure in heaven; and come, *follow me*" (Matt. 19:21, emphasis added). The young man's face fell, and he went away sad. What was the reason for his sadness? He had many possessions and was overly attached to them, preferring them to Jesus Christ. Never again does he appear in the Gospels.

In a society with an overabundance of things, to become attached inordinately to material things can happen almost imperceptibly. Judas Iscariot fell in love with money and fell out of love with Jesus Christ. Ananias and Sapphira, whom we find in the Acts of the Apostles, were struck dead on account of their insatiable desire for earthly things (Acts 5:1–10).

A striking parable, related to the dangers of greed, is the parable of Lazarus and the rich man (Luke 16:19–31). The poor man, Lazarus, covered with sores, sits outside the gate of the rich man's house day and night. In contrast, the rich man, dressed in fine purple, feasts sumptuously every day. Never once does he lift his hand to offer Lazarus as much as a piece of bread. After their deaths, the rich man finds himself in the fiery torments of hell, longing for a drop of water to refresh his tongue. The poor man, Lazarus, rests in the bosom of Abraham. What was the principle reason for the eternal loss of the rich man? It was not for anything that he *did* (sins of commission); rather, it was what he *failed* to do (sins of omission). His greed had blinded him totally to poor Lazarus outside his gate.

How, then, can you conquer the sin of greed that might be lurking or hiding in the depths of your soul? Here are some concrete steps to help you win the battle:

Admit it and confess it.

If you have detected greed as an insidious worm gnawing away at your interior life, then admit it, confess it, and beg for healing. Jesus is the spiritual physician of our soul. He has come to heal the wounds of our sins.

Meditate on the Life of Christ.

Follow this thumbnail sketch of Christ's life:

- He was born of poor parents in a stable in Bethlehem.

- He worked as a carpenter.

- He suffered forty days and nights in the desert fasting from food and drink.

- He went three years without a permanent abode. ("Foxes have holes, and birds of the air nests, but the Son of Man has nowhere to lay his head" [Matt. 8:20].)

- He was stripped of his garments and scourged.

- He was nailed to a cross and abandoned by almost everyone.

- He died and poured out his precious blood.

- He was buried in a borrowed tomb.

Recalling how the Son of the living God himself lived poorly and detached from material things can help transform your spiritual perspective, your outlook on material reality, and the attitude of your heart.

Remember the Life to Come.

One day you must die and be judged by Jesus, and heaven or hell awaits you. Look at your many possessions, and consider whether they will be a stepping stone to heaven for all eternity?

St. Francis Borgia, S.J., who had been the Duke of Gandía, had admired the beautiful queen, who died suddenly. At the funeral, as he followed the queen's casket, the lid popped open, and Francis saw this most beautiful woman's face being eaten by worms. After meditating on the transitory reality of beauty and wealth, Francis left all to enter the religious life and become a Jesuit priest and a great saint.

Although possessions are not sinful in themselves, our attachments to them can lead us to concentrate only on this life instead of on the glorious, heavenly life with Christ, a king surpassing all earthly royalty. We might need possessions to live in this life, but they shouldn't distract us from the life to come.

Learn to Give Generously.

St. Paul challenges us to remember "the words of the Lord Jesus, how he said, 'It is more blessed to give than to receive'" (Acts 20:35).

Blessed Teresa of Calcutta, who gave all away to follow Jesus in serving the indigent, encouraged us to "give until it hurts." Her lifelong desire was to quench the thirst of Jesus by serving the poorest of the poor. For her, Jesus was truly present in the "distressing disguise of the poor."

Do not worry, but trust in God's providential care.

In the Sermon of the Mount, Jesus warns us not to worry, especially about material things, such as food and clothing. Look at the birds of the air and the lilies of the field. God watches over them (cf. Matt. 6:26). The key is in these words of Jesus: "[S]trive first for the kingdom of God and his righteousness, and all these things will be given to you as well" (Matt. 6:33). Remember: if you receive Jesus in Holy Communion, you indeed are the richest of all. Having God living within the depths of your soul is already living out the Kingdom of God that is truly within. "If God is for us, who is against us?" (Rom. 8:31). Recall Psalm 23:1: "The Lord is my shepherd, I shall not want."

20

Suffering for a Purpose

In and of itself, suffering has no positive value. One thing can change that: uniting our suffering with that of our Lord and Savior Jesus Christ. As Christ had to endure great suffering while on earth, we can easily see our physical and emotional suffering in him, and we know that he unites himself with all of humanity in this. We do not have to like our suffering, but we can unite it with Christ's and see how He can bring grace out of our troubles. Only when this divine connection has been established does human suffering have positive value. Indeed, without this connection, suffering can make us bitter.

Jesus never promised his followers that they would be free from suffering. On the contrary, he stated: "If any man would come after me, let him deny himself and take up his cross and follow me" (Matt. 16:24). Taking up the cross is another way of saying accepting the reality of suffering in one's life.

Jesus did not simply preach the reality of suffering and its value, but he also put into practice what he preached. He did not flee from suffering or even the Cross. He suffered the many and painful aspects of his passion not only to obey the will of the heavenly Father, but also to show to us how much he loves each of us. How great is the love of God and his willingness to suffer to the point of shedding his precious blood for our eternal salvation.

How, then, can you take advantage of your suffering so that it will transform you not into a bitter person but rather into a much better person?

Contemplate the Passion of Christ.

Make it a habit to contemplate the suffering and death of Jesus frequently. Once a week, perhaps each Friday, spend some time in silent prayer and meditation on one aspect of the passion of Christ — perhaps his lonely agony in the Garden of Gethsemane; or the wounds on his back from the scourging; or one of the many thorns that pierced his sacred brow; or the nail that pierced one of his hands; or his precious blood draining out of his wounds as he hung valiantly on the Cross. Contemplate any detail that moves you to love the Lord Jesus more intensely.

Resign Yourself to God's Will.

When God deigns to send you suffering in whatever form it might be, strive to accept the suffering immediately with trust and confidence, with the full awareness that Jesus purposely has sent this suffering to you because he loves you and wants you to share, to a limited degree, in his suffering. Whatever God sends you is always for your benefit and well-being. Remember this principle of St. Augustine: God can allow what appears to be evil — various forms of suffering — to bring a greater good out of it.

Beg for Grace.

It is not wrong to beg to be freed from suffering. In his agony in the garden, Jesus begged the Father three times to take from him the chalice of suffering, but always with the concluding words,

"[N]ot my will, but thine, be done" (Luke 22:42). If God deems it best not to take that cross from you, then he will bring greater blessings from it. God sees what you can't—the whole picture. In the light of the salvation of your soul and of eternity, God has allowed that cross for your purification, sanctification, and eternal salvation. So ask God for the grace to bear the suffering with acceptance.

Unite Your Suffering to the Mass.

At every celebration of the holy sacrifice of the Mass, Jesus offers himself as the spotless victim for the salvation of the world. To maximize the value of your own suffering, place it on the altar during the Mass: at the moment of Consecration, when the body of Jesus is being elevated, mentally offer your sufferings with Jesus. Then, when you receive Holy Communion, having offered your sufferings to Jesus and with Jesus, countless graces and blessings will flow upon you, your family, the Church, and the world.

Offer Up Your Sufferings.

Your sufferings might seem too much to bear, and you might have trouble not thinking about them. Instead, offer your sufferings up for your own soul and for the intentions of your loved ones. This will allow you to carry your cross while also using it to help redeem yourself and bring goodness into the lives of those around you. In this, you will truly unite yourself to Christ.

Pray to Our Lady of Sorrows.

After Jesus, nobody ever suffered to the extent of Mary, the Mother of God, who has been called Our Lady of Sorrows. She bore and raised Jesus into adulthood only to see him suffer unto death. Her Immaculate Heart has endured great suffering but also experienced great glory. In your sufferings — physical, emotional, family, economic, moral, or even spiritual — turn to Our Lady of Sorrows and place all in her Immaculate Heart. Who better than our own Mother Mary to speak to when we feel overwhelmed? She can hear you and be a refuge for you, but, more than that, she knows better than any other human person how our God can bring good out of evil and give meaning to our sufferings. Mary will tell you: nobody suffers without a purpose, and there is a great and holy work being done in you.

Through her powerful prayers, Our Lady of Sorrows will turn your thorn into a rose, your storm into a rainbow, your death into life, and Good Friday shall give way to the glory of Jesus, our resurrected Lord.

In conclusion, let us all come to terms with the inevitable and unavoidable reality of human suffering. Let us not waste it but rather unite it to the passion and death of Jesus with the firm conviction and limitless hope that suffering united with Jesus purifies, elevates, ennobles, and sanctifies. In this way, our suffering will not make us bitter individuals but better ones.

We adore you, O Christ, and we bless you, because by your holy Cross you have redeemed the world.

21

Forming a Healthy Conscience

God has endowed us all with consciences, and it is our obliga-tion to work at forming them. Simply following the flow of the world and worldly values, especially as communicated by the mass media, is no way to form our consciences. On the contrary, often the values we find on TV, in movies, and on talk shows are antithetical to true Christian values.

Many people assert, "I must follow my own conscience." Or: "I have to be true to myself." Or: "I feel that this is what is right for me." All of these statements affirm what Pope Benedict XVI warned us frequently to avoid: the dictatorship of relativism. Pope Benedict cautioned us not to follow the flow, or our feel-ings, or the modern current of worldly values, or subjectivism, but rather to pursue truth—absolute truth, which is found not so much in a philosophical system, but in a person: Jesus Christ, the son of the living God, who said, "I am the way, and the truth, and the life" (John 14:6).

One of the most basic principles, instilled in every human person who enters the world, is "Do good and avoid evil." How-ever, due to shattered families, neo-paganism, Freudianism, and a growing hedonism in the modern world, many are brought up without any moral compass whatsoever. Their consciences have never been properly formed. In time, they can even be *de*formed or, worse, killed. God respects our freedom, which we can choose to use for his honor and glory or to abuse for our own condemnation.

It is incumbent upon all to work at forming a healthy conscience — or better yet, what we call a "delicate conscience." Call to mind the immortal words of Pope Pius XII: "Perhaps the greatest sin in the world today is that men have begun to lose the sense of sin."[28] As a priest and confessor, I find that the person who scares me most — with regard to the salvation of his immortal soul — is the individual who arrogantly brags that he actually has no sin. Why is he so scary? For the simple reason that the purpose of the incarnation, of Jesus' life among us, and especially of his excruciating passion and death and his resurrection, was precisely to forgive our sins, to redeem us, to ransom us from the enemy, and to conquer the devil. As Fulton Sheen highlights, Jesus is our teacher, but more important, he is our savior and redeemer.

Let us consider the types of conscience and how to form them better:

Erroneous Conscience

An *erroneous* conscience is one that is wrapped in error, falsehoods, and lies. Many of us, even those who are ardently pursuing authentic holiness, still have some blind spots in the formation of our conscience.

---

[28] Pope Pius XII, Radio message of His Holiness Pius XII to participants in the National Catechetical Congress of the United States, Boston, October 26, 1946.

This conscience is best remedied by forming the soul through the precepts of the Church and sacred scripture. Try reading St. Augustine's *Confessions* and see how he slowly formed his ideas about right and wrong and eventually converted.

Deformed Conscience

A *deformed* conscience is one that was once well formed but, due to a lack of proper ongoing formation, and to mental and spiritual laziness, gradually lost its light and became filled with errors, prejudices, and false ideas. This conscience might be compared to a once manicured garden that, left untended for six months, becomes filled with ugly weeds and ravenous insects. The conscience must be cultivated, or, like this garden, it will be cluttered with weeds of immorality.

The cure for this conscience is proper, ongoing formation. Seek a spiritual director, and read the *Catechism*. Attend daily Mass and ask for the Holy Spirit to guide you to a proper understanding of what is right and what it wrong.

Lax Conscience

A *lax* conscience has lost most of its light; just a flicker, a minute flame, still exists. A person with a lax conscience experiences remorse only when he commits the most egregious of sins. How often have I heard this comment: "I'm a good person! I don't kill, and I don't steal." This statement summarizes this type of conscience. It reacts only to the most horrendous of sins but is blind to so many other moral transgressions. Remember: the farther we walk away from the light, the less we can see the coffee spots on our white shirt.

To improve a lax conscience, contemplate the saints who were aware of their faults and embrace and imitate their humility.

Consider, as an example, the Angelic Doctor, Thomas Aquinas, who prayed, "If I have taught anything false, I leave correction of it to the Roman Catholic Church."[29]

Scrupulous Conscience

A *scrupulous* conscience tends to perceive sin where sin actually does not exist or to blow the gravity of sin out of proportion. At the same time, a person who has a scrupulous conscience can be totally blind to objectively grave sins. Sts. Maximilian Kolbe and Thérèse of Lisieux passed through a stage of scrupulosity. St. Ignatius himself, shortly after his conversion in the Battle of Pamplona and after having painstakingly made his general confession — which took several days — suffered severe scrupulosity.

How, then, can one resolve such a state of soul? Very simply: obedience. The scrupulous conscience must be sincere and transparent to his confessor and obey all of his advice and counsel. Through obedience, the soul will find peace.

Doubtful or Perplexed Conscience

A person with a *doubtful* or *perplexed* conscience may find himself in a moral predicament in which he cannot find a clear answer. He may have to decide between two alternatives, but it seems to him that either one of the decisions carries with it moral guilt.

A basic principle of moral theology applies to this predicament: you should never act on a "doubtful conscience." That is because one must never risk offending God through sin. What is

---

[29] St. Thomas Aquinas, trans. R. Anderson and J. Moser, *The Aquinas Prayer Book* (Manchester: Sophia Institute Press, 2000), 113.

the solution to this predicament? Seek out counsel, either from a competent confessor or spiritual director or by consulting a good manual on moral theology that clearly addresses and responds to the moral dilemma at hand. In other words, God never pushes us into sin. As St. Paul asserts, "God is faithful, and he will not let you be tempted beyond your strength, but with the temptation will also provide the way of escape, that you may be able to endure it" (1 Cor. 10:13). The problem is not God, but our lack of collaboration with his grace.

Dead Conscience

A *dead* conscience is one that has not been developed, that has lain fallow, collected moral weeds that choked its voice so that it could no longer be heard, and has suffocated.

I once heard of a woman who had undergone twenty-eight abortions. I imagine that after the first abortion the woman had remorse of conscience, as well as after the second. But during the third, a gentle but insistent voice beckoned the poor woman to repentance and trust. However, after the tenth, no doubt, the conscience was silent. We can assassinate our conscience. Through repetition of sin, and increased gravity of the sin, and rejection of God's call to conversion, the conscience becomes calloused, cauterized, and it dies.

Guilty Conscience

A *guilty* conscience is not bad, if it is a correct one. To sweep sin under the rug does not resolve the problem but magnifies it. A bandage does not necessarily heal the cut. Iodine, disinfectant, and medical treatment are necessary for healing. A guilty conscience must come to terms with the sin, humbly admit it, confess it, and trust in God's mercy. Shakespeare presents Lady

Macbeth constantly washing her hands, a clear manifestation of guilt not resolved. All the waters of all the seas could not cleanse her from her guilt — only God's infinite mercy could.

Healthy or Correct Conscience

A *healthy* or *correct* conscience is what everyone should aim to attain in his spiritual life. This conscience reacts correctly to one's actions. When he acts virtuously, his conscience is filled with peace. However, when he does evil, sadness and remorse follow.

Delicate Conscience

A *delicate* conscience is above and beyond a healthy conscience. A person who has a delicate conscience is truly pursuing sanctity of life, abhors sin in all forms and degrees, and wants to go beyond the minimum. He desires the Ignatian "Magis": to give the Lord all that he is and has, to the utmost. This gem of a person strives to be attentive to even the slightest and most delicate inspirations of the Holy Spirit and to respond generously and immediately. When he fails to respond, the Holy Spirit gently but firmly notifies him of his failure.

Enlightened Conscience

An *enlightened* conscience is one on which God's light shines. A person with an enlightened conscience seeks true light in the word of God, in the Magisterium of the Church, in the teachings of the popes, their documents and especially their encyclicals, and in the lives, writings, and examples of the saints, all of which reflect the virtues of Jesus Christ.

Imagine a room with a window facing to the sun at midday. Picture these different scenarios:

1. The window and its shutters are closed, and the shade is drawn — the room is in total darkness.

2. The shutters and the shade are partly opened. A streak of sunlight passes through the window. Mere objects can be detected.

3. The shutters and the shade are half open, so that objects can be seen but without any detail observed.

4. The window and shutters are open, and the shade is up. The sun pours forth its rays, penetrating and inundating the room. The chairs, tables, and bed can be seen down to the most minute detail. Not only that, but even the tiny dust particles floating in the room can be seen.

This analogy of the room applies to our conscience. All have a conscience, given as a gift by our loving God. However, some have an erroneous conscience, others a lax one, still others might have deformed their conscience to the point of cauterizing or even killing it. Those of goodwill recognize the reality of sin and that it is part of our fallen human nature and therefore take specific steps to know themselves and the truth in the light of God's word, as explained by the Magisterium and the teachings of the Holy Father. They have acquired a healthy or even delicate conscience.

May our consciences be like the room open to divine sunlight so that God's light of truth will illuminate us and set us free.

22

Confession

Confession is the sacrament of the Church by which we are reconciled to God and delivered from our sins, restoring perfect friendship with Jesus. The better you prepare for Confession, the more abundant the graces you will receive and the greater the peace in your soul will be.

Following are ten practices that will help you make better confessions.

Resolve to Receive the Sacrament Well.

Two of the most important actions we can accomplish as Catholics are to go to Confession and to receive Holy Communion. In these sacraments we have a direct contact with our Lord and Savior Jesus Christ. This being the case, we should make a concerted effort to improve our encounters with Jesus in these sacraments. In other words, we should never take these sacraments for granted.

Also, be keenly aware of the concept of *dispositive grace*. The abundance of graces are received in direct proportion to the disposition of the recipient. There was a time when a young priest would often see on the walls of the sanctuary: "Dear priest of God, say this Mass as if it were your first Mass, your last Mass, and your only Mass."[30] We can apply the same principle to Confession: "Confess as if it were your first, last, and only confession."

Pray before Your Confession.

One way to receive abundant grace is by appealing to the Communion of Saints, so pray to the holy confessors to help you to make a good confession. Here are a few: the Curé of Ars (St. John Marie Vianney), St. John Bosco, St. Leonard of Port Maurice, St. Leopold Mandic, St. Pio of Pietrelcina, St. Francis Regis, St. Alphonsus Liguori, St. Anthony Claret, and St. Ignatius of Loyola. To borrow again from the Beatles: "You'll get by with a little help from your friends." Pray to them (to the saints, not to the Beatles!) to help you to confess well and that each confession you make will be better than your prior confession.

Prepare the Night Before.

Use a good examination-of-conscience booklet or guide. Find a quiet and contemplative place to examine your conscience. Use a crucifix and the Divine Mercy image to elicit sorrow and trust. Write down your sins so that, as so often happens, you do not forget them when you're in the confessional. Also, pray for your confessor — to his guardian angel — before you enter the confessional.

Develop Self-Knowledge.

One of the classical steps to making a good confession is to have a *firm purpose of amendment*. This entails rewinding the film of your

---

[30] Cf. Sara E. Shea, *Father John's Story* (Raleigh, NC: Lulu Press, 2012), 36; *Powerful Prayers Every Catholic Should Know*, ed. Bud MacFarlane and Tim Harrison (Fairview Park, OH: Mary Foundation, 2013), 12.

life and seeing the various ways you fell into sin and what were the causes that led to the sin. Maybe it is a person who jeopardizes your spiritual life. Maybe it is a recurring situation at work or in your family. Maybe it is your physical state of weariness. It might be an improper use of electronic media and a lack of prudence. You will often notice a pattern that leads to the slippery path and collapse. For this reason the faithful observance of what the *Spiritual Exercises* calls the "Daily Examen" can be a valuable tool to help you know yourself and to avoid the near occasion of sin.

Read Biblical Passages to Help You Prepare.

The Church highly recommends the use of sacred scripture as a means to prepare for a better reception of the sacraments. Two excellent passages I recommend are Luke 15 and Psalm 51. Luke 15 presents the parables of God's mercy, and the greatest is the parable of the prodigal son. Psalm 51 is one of the best acts of contrition ever composed, and by none other than King David himself (after he had committed adultery with Bathsheba and killed an innocent man).

Confess Frequently.

The saints highly recommend frequent Confession as a most efficacious means of growing in sanctifying grace. Confession either restores sanctifying grace or augments it. Of course, this presupposes a thorough preparation.

Receive Sacramental Grace.

Confession is a sacrament of healing, in which Jesus comes to us as the divine physician. The grace he gives us repairs, restores, and fortifies. Come to Jesus with all your spiritual wounds—and, indeed, there is no one else to turn to.

Develop the Qualities of a Good Confession.

In the *Diary* of St. Faustina the most important qualities of a good confession are highlighted in number 113: (1) complete sincerity and openness, (2) humility, and (3) obedience. By adhering to these qualities we cannot go wrong. Reminder: we want to strive to make better Communions and Confessions until the end of our lives.

Don't Be Discouraged.

Even though you might fall frequently, never give in to discouragement. We may have clung to some bad habits for decades. Too many people, unfortunately, have a "microwave" approach to spirituality; in other words, they want instant holiness. It does not work that way. Change is often tedious, laborious, and painful. The key is to keep praying, working, and fighting as a true soldier of Christ to be liberated from sin. A key message from the *Diary* is that the worst thing possible is to fail to trust in God's infinite mercy. As St. Paul reminds us, "where sin increased, grace abounded all the more" (Rom. 5:20).

Turn to Mary.

Never forget to invite Mary to be present in your preparation for Confession. Even ask her to enter with you into the confessional so that you can make the best confession in your life. Pope St. John Paul II called the great Marian sanctuaries (Lourdes, Fátima, and Guadalupe) "spiritual clinics." Lines of penitents wait to meet the merciful Jesus in the confessional in these sanctuaries. Among the many beautiful titles of Mary are Mother of Mercy, Mother of Good Counsel, and Health of the Sick. The maternal intercession of Mary is behind many powerful conversions.

23

Mercy

Both St. John Paul II and St. Faustina stated unequivocally that the greatest virtue or attribute of God is his infinite mercy. Throughout the Bible, but especially in the New Testament, and most specifically in the Gospels, we see displayed marvelously the mercy of God.

Jesus is the incarnation of the mercy of God. The examples are abundant. Jesus comes to the rescue of the woman caught in adultery, who was about to be stoned to death: "Let him who is without sin among you be the first to throw a stone at her" (John 8:7). He forgives a woman who had been a prostitute and had been possessed by seven demons, who may in fact be the woman we know as St. Mary Magdalene. He forgives Zacchaeus, the tax collector, who showed his repentance by promising to give half his money to the poor and repay fourfold anybody he might have defrauded.

Now let us focus on what I think is a truly breathtaking manifestation of Jesus' mercy: the conversion of the good thief, related in Luke 23:33–43. You know the story well, no doubt, but I humbly offer some points for meditation:

The good thief had lived a very sinful life up to that moment. He was associated with stealing, killing, and was a revolutionary responsible for starting conflicts. This good thief, by being with Jesus, was transformed.

He heard Jesus forgive: "Father, forgive them, for they know not what they do" (Luke 23:34). The first words of Jesus on the Cross were of mercy and forgiveness. Mercy is the love of God forgiving the sinner. It is always available. The thief's heart was softened by the sacred and merciful heart of Jesus. The thief humbly and with a contrite heart begged for forgiveness. "Jesus, remember me when you come in your kingly power" (Luke 23:42). He thus became the first canonized saint, as the merciful Savior responded: "Truly, I say to you, today you will be with me in Paradise" (Luke 23:43).

Jesus is so merciful that his heart is always moved instantly to forgive a repentant heart. The repentant thief was forgiven in a heartbeat. "God is slow to anger and quick to forgive" (cf. Exod. 34:6). We should try to be slow to anger, rich in mercy, and quick to forgive.

Following are some meditations on the Divine Mercy of Christ:

God's Rich Mercy

God's greatest attribute is his mercy. No matter how grave and numerous our sins, God is always ready and willing to forgive us if we simply say: "Jesus, I am sorry. Forgive me." In a heartbeat Jesus is ready to forgive even the worst of sinners. Pope Francis says: "God never tires in forgiving us, but we become tired of asking for forgiveness."[31]

---

[31] Pope Francis, Angelus, March 17, 2013.

Our Need to Be Merciful

If we want to receive the mercy of God, we in turn must be merciful and be willing to forgive those who have hurt us. Jesus teaches us: "Be merciful, even as your Father is merciful" (Luke 6:36). The most renowned prayer in the world also reminds us: "Forgive us our trespasses as we forgive those who trespass against us." To receive God's mercy, we must be merciful, not just seven times, but seventy times seven times (cf. Matt. 18:22) — meaning always.

Confession

God's mercy is manifested most abundantly in our soul when we have recourse to Confession, the sacrament of God's mercy. Jesus expresses mercy in the person of the priest. If you have not been to confession in years, return. Jesus, the merciful Savior, is gently and patiently waiting for you. (See also chapter 22.)

The Hour of Mercy

The Hour of Mercy is 3:00 p.m. It is the hour when Jesus died. If possible, try to remember this moment every day and offer to the Father the dying Savior in his last agony for the salvation of the world, and especially for those who in that hour or on that day are in their last agony. God the Father will never deny his dying Son anything, nor will he deny those who unite themselves to his agony.

The Chaplet of Divine Mercy

The Chaplet of Divine Mercy is a beautiful prayer and can be prayed in a few minutes. In this prayer we offer to the Father his beloved Son — body, blood, soul, and divinity. Also we beg for the salvation of all the souls throughout the world. We should love what God loves; God has a burning thirst for the salvation of souls. Remember the motto of the great St. John Bosco: Give me souls and take all the rest away.

The Divine Mercy Novena

The Divine Mercy Novena starts on Good Friday and ends on Divine Mercy Sunday. The prayer intentions are a model for anybody who sincerely desires to learn the prayer of intercession. Even though this novena, properly speaking, is prayed over nine days, it can be prayed at any time and in any place.

Daily Act of Mercy

In St. Faustina's *Diary*, Jesus encourages us to understand mercy and to put it into practice every day, even in very small ways. Here are three ways to practice mercy:

- *Prayer.* By simply praying for the well-being of another person, you are already practicing mercy.

- *Words of kindness.* Get into the habit of speaking to others using kind words, a kind tone of voice, and kind gestures. A kind word can lift a soul in deep desolation into peace and consolation.

- *Deeds.* Support your kind words with deeds of loving kindness. Practice the Corporal Works of Mercy based on Matthew 25: feed the hungry, give drink to the thirsty, clothe the naked, shelter the homeless, visit the sick, visit the imprisoned, and bury the dead. What you do to others you are really doing to Jesus: "Truly, I say to you, as you did it to one of the least of these my brethren, you did it to me" (Matt. 25:40).

The Image of Divine Mercy

Jesus commanded St. Faustina to have an image or painting of him done. After being approved by her superior and spiritual director, the painting was accomplished. At first, the nun was displeased because she complained that Jesus himself was much more beautiful. But Jesus told her that his grace would still flow through the image. Enthroning an image of Divine Mercy in your home is an exterior sign that you desire that Jesus the king of mercy will reign there.

Divine Mercy Sunday

Divine Mercy Sunday falls the Sunday after Easter, and Jesus ardently desires that this feast be celebrated with special solemnity and that on that day the Divine Mercy image should be publically exposed, honored, and venerated. Pope John Paul II was instrumental in instituting this solemnity. It is not by chance that Pope John Paul II was canonized on Divine Mercy Sunday 2014, along with Pope John XXIII. Pope John Paul II taught Divine Mercy especially in his encyclical *Dives Misericordia* (*Rich in Mercy*). Equally important, this great modern saint lived mercy by forgiving the man who had tried to kill him on May 13, 1981.

Promise

One of the most exalted promises of Divine Mercy is that those who make a good, heartfelt, and contrite confession within eight days before or after Divine Mercy Sunday and receive the Holy Eucharist will receive forgiveness for all their sins as well as the temporal punishment due to those sins.[32] In other words, their souls will return to the state of baptismal innocence. And if

[32] See https://www.ewtn.com/Devotionals/mercy/summary.htm.

anyone who had fulfilled those conditions were to die in that moment, his soul would fly directly to heaven. How sublime is the mercy of God.

Apostle of Divine Mercy

Become an apostle of Divine Mercy. Read St. Faustina's *Diary* to become familiar with the message. Live out mercy in your life by forgiving immediately and from your heart. Try to pray the Divine Mercy Chaplet at the bedside of anyone who is in his last agony. Jesus has promised to have mercy on that soul and on the souls of all who seek forgiveness for their sins, no matter how much those sins might cause them to despair. God's mercy goes way beyond our understanding.

Mary and Mercy

Love Mary. St. Alphonsus Liguori states that in God there is both mercy and justice. However, Mary is the essence and the embodiment of mercy. That is why we pray as such, *"Hail Holy Queen, mother of mercy, our life our sweetness and our hope . . .*

If we understand mercy, strive to live out mercy, promote mercy in all times and circumstances, and die trusting in God's mercy, then the merciful Savior, when we die, will say: "Well done, good and faithful servant;... enter into the joy of your master" (Matt. 25:21).

24

Go Set the World on Fire

The last words that St. Ignatius of Loyola addressed to his dear friend, Francis Xavier, before sending him on one of the greatest missionary enterprises in the history of Christianity, were "Go set the world on fire!"

St. Benedict Joseph Labre said that we need always to have a "heart of fire" for God.[33] These exhortations and assertions flow from the Master Himself, who exclaimed: "I came to cast fire upon the earth; and would that it were already kindled!" (Luke 12:49). One of the prayers in the Litany of the Sacred Heart of Jesus is: "Sacred Heart of Jesus, burning furnace of charity, have mercy on us."

We must not forget that, after nine days of prayer with the Blessed Virgin Mary in the upper room, the Holy Spirit descended on the apostles in tongues of fire. This fire of the Holy Spirit transformed these weak, irresolute, confused, and somewhat ignorant men into valiant soldiers of Christ, ready and willing to travel to the most distant and remote regions of the

---

[33] Jill Haak Adels, *The Wisdom of the Saints* (Oxford: Oxford University Press, 1987), 137.

earth to preach the gospel of Jesus Christ.[34] All of them—with the exception of the apostle St. John—sealed their lives with the glorious shedding of their blood in martyrdom. God's fire transformed them radically and permanently!

St. Philip Neri had his own Pentecost experience. After he had prayed and fasted for nine days in one of the catacombs of Rome, the Holy Spirit descended in the form of a ball of fire, entered his mouth, and descended into his heart. From that time on, Philip's heart would beat ferociously due to the fire of God's love in him.

Meditate on these examples of fire-filled Christians, and contrast them with the modern malady of religious indifference, one of the most widespread and pernicious signs of our times. Yes, there are hostile and antagonistic forces working against Jesus and his Church—there always have been and always will be. Yet a quiet plague of indifference, tepidity, lukewarmness, a "whatever" attitude has permeated modern society. The Christian fire has been extinguished and the coals are smoldering, engendering mediocrity in the followers of our Lord and Savior Jesus Christ.

The Church is a sleeping giant. There are more than a billion Catholics spread throughout the world. How many of these are asleep, whether taking a siesta or in a comatose state? Where is that fire?

How does God view this lack of fire? How does God look down from heaven on the indifferent? The words from the book of Revelation should penetrate us to the very depths of our hearts: "[Y]ou have abandoned the love you had at first.... [R]epent and do the works you did at first. If not, I will come to you and remove your lampstand from its place" (Luke 2:4–5).

---

[34] See Acts 2.

Remember the fervor you experienced the day of your First Communion? Has that fervor all but died out in your heart?

Also from Revelation: "I know your works: you are neither cold nor hot. Would that you were cold or hot! So, because you are lukewarm, and neither cold nor hot, I will spew you out of my mouth" (Rev. 3:15–16).

How can we conquer our indifference? How can we rise out of our lukewarmness and cease living as mediocre Christians, as smoldering wicks on the verge of being snuffed out completely? What is the remedy?

Let me give one simple suggestion. To keep a bonfire burning, the key is to keep feeding the flames. Brushwood, dry leaves, twigs, and branches must be constantly cast into the fire, or it will die. Similarly, we must fan the flame in our spiritual lives.

Don't just imagine the fire of the Holy Spirit. Beg him for your own personal Pentecost experience. It is never too late. God is always ready and waiting patiently for well-disposed, humble, and docile hearts.

If the apostles could receive that fire, if St. Francis Xavier was commissioned to ignite flames, if St. Philip Neri was consumed to the very depths of his heart with Pentecost fire, then why can't we open our hearts here and now to receive that same fire?

God gives. The nature of God's essence is utter goodness and self-giving. God *loves* to give. He gave his only son for us to save us for all eternity. God still longs to give to us. We will more quickly tire of receiving God's gifts than God will tire of giving them to us.

Jesus gave a special gift that Easter evening when the apostles were in the upper room. The risen Lord came through the door and greeted the apostles with these words: "Peace be with you.... Receive the Holy Spirit" (John 20:21, 22).

As the Holy Spirit rushed impetuously on David at his anointing by the prophet Samuel (see 1 Sam. 16:13), may the Holy Spirit rush upon us. As Jesus breathed forth the Holy Spirit on the apostles, may he breathe on us. As the Holy Spirit descended on the apostles in tongues of fire on Pentecost, may we receive at least a spark of that same Holy Spirit.

May our Lady come to our aid. Mary is the daughter of the eternal Father, the Mother of the divine son, and the mystical spouse of the Holy Spirit. Let us implore her intercession: *Come Holy Spirit, come, through the heart of Mary.*

About the Author
Fr. Ed Broom, O.M.V.

Fr. Ed Broom, O.M.V., had the privilege of being ordained by Pope St. John Paul II on Trinity Sunday, May 25, 1986. He worked in South America during his first years as a priest and in Los Angeles for the past twenty-three years.

As an Oblate of the Virgin Mary, Fr. Broom is dedicated to giving the *Spiritual Exercises* of Saint Ignatius of Loyola, to promoting Marian devotion and consecration, and to promoting God's infinite mercy through the sacrament of Confession. He also strives to preach the word of God through electronic media, including YouTube, Facebook, podcasts, and blog articles in English and Spanish.

Sophia Institute

Sophia Institute is a nonprofit institution that seeks to nurture the spiritual, moral, and cultural life of souls and to spread the Gospel of Christ in conformity with the authentic teachings of the Roman Catholic Church.

Sophia Institute Press fulfills this mission by offering translations, reprints, and new publications that afford readers a rich source of the enduring wisdom of mankind.

Sophia Institute also operates two popular online Catholic resources: CrisisMagazine.com and CatholicExchange.com.

Crisis Magazine provides insightful cultural analysis that arms readers with the arguments necessary for navigating the ideological and theological minefields of the day. *Catholic Exchange* provides world news from a Catholic perspective as well as daily devotionals and articles that will help you to grow in holiness and live a life consistent with the teachings of the Church.

In 2013, Sophia Institute launched Sophia Institute for Teachers to renew and rebuild Catholic culture through service to Catholic education. With the goal of nurturing the spiritual, moral, and cultural life of souls, and an abiding respect for the role and work of teachers, we strive to provide materials and programs that are at once enlightening to the mind and ennobling to the heart; faithful and complete, as well as useful and practical.

Sophia Institute gratefully recognizes the Solidarity Association for preserving and encouraging the growth of our apostolate over the course of many years. Without their generous and timely support, this book would not be in your hands.

www.SophiaInstitute.com
www.CatholicExchange.com
www.CrisisMagazine.com
www.SophiaInstituteforTeachers.org

Sophia Institute Press® is a registered trademark of Sophia Institute.
Sophia Institute is a tax-exempt institution as defined by the Internal Revenue Code, Section 501(c)(3). Tax I.D. 22-2548708.